proud to be the dabbers

celebrating 125 years of Nantwich Town Football Club
1884-2009

by
michael chatwin

mpire

Front Cover: Nantwich's 1896 Cheshire Junior Cup winning side and below (from left to right) a fan at the 2006 FA Vase Final, Phil Parkinson captain of the 2008 Cheshire Senior Cup winning side, Peter Hall and Steve Davis with the FA Vase, 2008/09 leading scorer Michael Lennon.

First published in the United Kingdom by
Empire, 4 Market Street, Nantwich, Cheshire. CW5 5DJ.

ISBN 978-0-9563068-0-7

Copyright © Michael Chatwin, 2009

First published: July 2009

All rights reserved. This publication may not be reproduced, stored in a retrieval system, or transmitted, in any form or by any means electronic, mechanical, photocopying, recording or otherwise, without the prior permission of the publishers.

Book Design & Origination by Michael Chatwin

Printed by HSW Print - (01443) 441100

introduction

125 years is a long time in anyone's book. For a club like Nantwich Town to have survived since 1884 is a great achievement and then to have so prospered over recent years is a tribute to those who have served the club over a century and a quarter.

When I wrote the club's Centenary history some 25 years ago, little could I have anticipated the changes that were to come. The club has progressed immeasurably, both on and off the field, since those days in the Second Division of the North West Counties League. I myself moved away from the area and, on my return, was honoured to serve as club President. Like many, I watched our thrilling FA Vase Final win at St Andrews with great pride. The move to The Weaver Stadium which soon followed triggered further success, success which could hardly have been contemplated back in 1984. I wonder what our founders of 1884 would make of it all.

History, as they say, is forever changing and open to interpretation. Endless hours poring over microfilm of old newspapers has been the primary source of information for me, peppered with personal anecdotes and memories. Like many smaller clubs, Nantwich's fortunes have not been particularly well documented over the years and I apologise for any inaccuracies which may appear. Corrections or amendments that I am made aware of will be posted on the website for the book - www.ProudToBeTheDabbers.co.uk.

In compiling this book, I have attempted to present a flavour of the club over the years, picking out some of its highs and lows and painting pictures of the personalities who have helped mould it. I have tried to avoid getting bogged down in statistics and records. The internet is a great place for holding such data and so, from time to time, I have noted where a surfer can

Michael Chatwin (left) with Jon Brydon (Vice Chairman), Clare Wilson (Crewe & Nantwich Borough Council), Clive Jackson (Chairman) and John Ackerley (Cheshire FA) at the announcement of the £1 million Football Foundation grant for the new stadium in February 2004.

access relevant information. Having said that, it would be nice, at some point, to publish a complete record of the club's results and scorers. That task is for another time but should it see light of day, you will also be able to find out about it at www.ProudToBeTheDabbers.co.uk

Putting together this book has been something of a labour of love for me. However, it would not have been possible without the help and support of many others and for this I am most grateful. 128 pages can never be enough to do justice to 125 years of history, so apologies also for events or names that may have been omitted. Not withstanding that, I hope the pages that follow evoke some warm memories of a club that has most certainly stood the greatest test of all - the test of time.

MICHAEL CHATWIN
July 2009

JIMMY QUINN

Born Belfast, 18 November 1959
Playing Career Whitchurch Alport, Nantwich Town, Congleton Town, Oswestry Town
Dec 1981 (£10,000) SWINDON TOWN 34 League appearances +15 as substitute, 10 League goals
Aug 1984 (£32,500) BLACKBURN ROVERS 58+13, 17
Dec 1986 (£50,000) SWINDON TOWN 61+3, 30
Jun 1988 (£210,000) LEICESTER CITY 13+18, 6
Mar 1989 (£210,000) BRADFORD CITY 35, 14
Dec 1989 (£320,000) WEST HAM UNITED 34+13, 18
Aug 1991 (£40,000) BOURNEMOUTH 43, 19
July 1992 (£55,000) READING 149+33, 71
July 1997 PETERBOROUGH UNITED 47+2, 25
Nov 1999 SWINDON TOWN 1+6
Weymouth, Cirencester Town, Nantwich Town, Northwich Victoria, Hereford United, Highworth Town, Hayes, Congleton Town, Northwich Victoria, Shrewsbury Town, Nantwich Town.
Northern Ireland 48 caps, 12 goals.
Managerial career Reading, Swindon Town, Northwich Victoria, Shrewsbury Town, Egersund IK, Cambridge United, Bournemouth.

foreword

For a football club to have battled to stay alive over the passage of 125 years is an achievement in itself. To have overcome adversity to prosper as it has in recent seasons is a massive achievement. Full credit to everyone who has pulled together to gain this success and credit also to those who steered the ship through stormy waters in times past.

Nantwich Town Football Club will always have a special place in my affections. Colin Hutchinson brought me to Jackson Avenue in the summer of 1979 as a lanky youngster who'd been playing for Whitchurch Alport. I made my debut in the opening game of the 1979/80 season. I'm told we beat Droylsden 1-0 but it's that long ago I don't really remember much about it!

It still seems remarkable to me that I was back on that old ground in 2006, coming off the bench in that famous semi against Cammell Laird to help the club towards FA Vase glory.

During those 27 years in between, I was lucky enough to have lived every schoolboy's dream. I had fantastic years at Blackburn Rovers, West Ham United and Reading. But nothing can beat playing football for your country and, for me, pulling on the Northern Ireland jersey (yes – green, of course!) was the pinnacle of my career.

For me the highs and lows of football management beckoned but I have always kept a close eye on the Dabbers. In applauding the achievements made over recent years, I acknowledge the devotion of those hard working people who, over the last century and a quarter, have made the club what it is today. This is their story, and we are grateful to Michael Chatwin for his dedication in bringing it to life for us.

Here's to the next 125 years,

Jimmy Quinn

in the beginning

$\mathcal{P}$icture yourself in old Nantwich in the 1880s. Queen Victoria is on the throne, England has yet to experience the Boer War, the concept of a World War is, as yet, unknown. The town itself has a population of just 7500 - a market town, of course, renowned for its salt and shoemaking. The clothing trade was just starting to come to the fore.

Nantwich, like the rest of England, is undergoing change. As industrialisation gathers pace, the face of the town changes but it is outstripped by neighbouring Crewe where the introduction of the railways fuels the town's population boom. The foul stench of untreated hides at Harvey's Tannery would fill your nostrils and churn your stomach, horses and carriages would clatter around the cobbled streets.

As in the rest of the country, the workers are looking for an outlet in their leisure time. Association football, originally the preserve of public schools and southern gents, is gaining credence as a game for workers; for proper men. And so it was in Nantwich.

Men from the town had taken up the challenge in December 1877. A club from that burgeoning new town down the road had recently been formed, so when Crewe Alexandra threw down the gauntlet, Nantwich put up a team to take them on and gained a creditable 0-0 draw.

The Alex soon established themselves as a force to be reckoned with in local circles but the loose association of players that had represented Nantwich went their separate ways as a clutch of clubs sprung up in the old town. Nantwich Church House, Nantwich Wanderers, Nantwich Rovers all played friendly matches against neighbouring clubs but it was not until 1884 that a club was formally organised to represent the town.

William Bullock
pictured around 1900

WILLIAM BULLOCK

Billy Bullock is believed to have been the club's first secretary and it is likely that he was involved in its formation. He played in Nantwich's first ever game and was a regular in the playing line-up until March 1892 when he broke his leg in a friendly match against Crewe Alexandra Hornets. He was a popular player but the severity of the injury forced his retirement from the game. Like most players of the time, he was not insured so the club granted him a benefit match. Over 3000 watched the game against Crewe Alexandra, played in April 1892, and the following year he became club treasurer. He again acted as secretary for the 1894/95 season. An accomplished cricketer, he tragically contracted pneumonia from which he died in January 1902, still in his 30s.

IN THE BEGINNING

And so Nantwich Football Club was born and, in September 1884, registered with the Cheshire Football Association. The founding fathers of the club included William Bullock who played for the club and is believed to have been the club's first secretary.

So the new Nantwich Football Club took to the field for the first time against Crewe Rovers in October 1884. Today's fans would hardly recognise the game as it was played then. No goal nets, of course, and no penalty kicks, either. There was less passing - certainly little long range passes - with the ball often being moved forward in 'scrimmages', almost like a scrum in rugby with players from both sides surrounding the ball and attempting to hack it forward. Games, themselves, were disorganised with goals being disputed - hardly surprising given the lack of nets. Disagreements would spill over into bad temper and, at times, spark aggression on the pitch and violence off it. No surprise, either, that results of matches were contested.

So it was with Nantwich's first ever game against Crewe Rovers - with the result being that Nantwich won by one goal and four disputed to nil. It was a dull and gloomy afternoon and a rough pitch didn't make for good football. Rovers were also short of a player - so one of the spectators was called on to make up the numbers!

The following Saturday, Nantwich were due to play Hanley but the visitors didn't even turn up so a game was arranged, at short notice, away to the old Nantwich Church House club. Played at Shrewbridge Park, the old Crewe Guardian reported that, "The Church House team was pressed to the extreme," and that "the Reverand M.F.Coates was very active in goal." Seemingly, nobody from above helped out the Church House team as the town team comfortably ran out 13-0 winners.

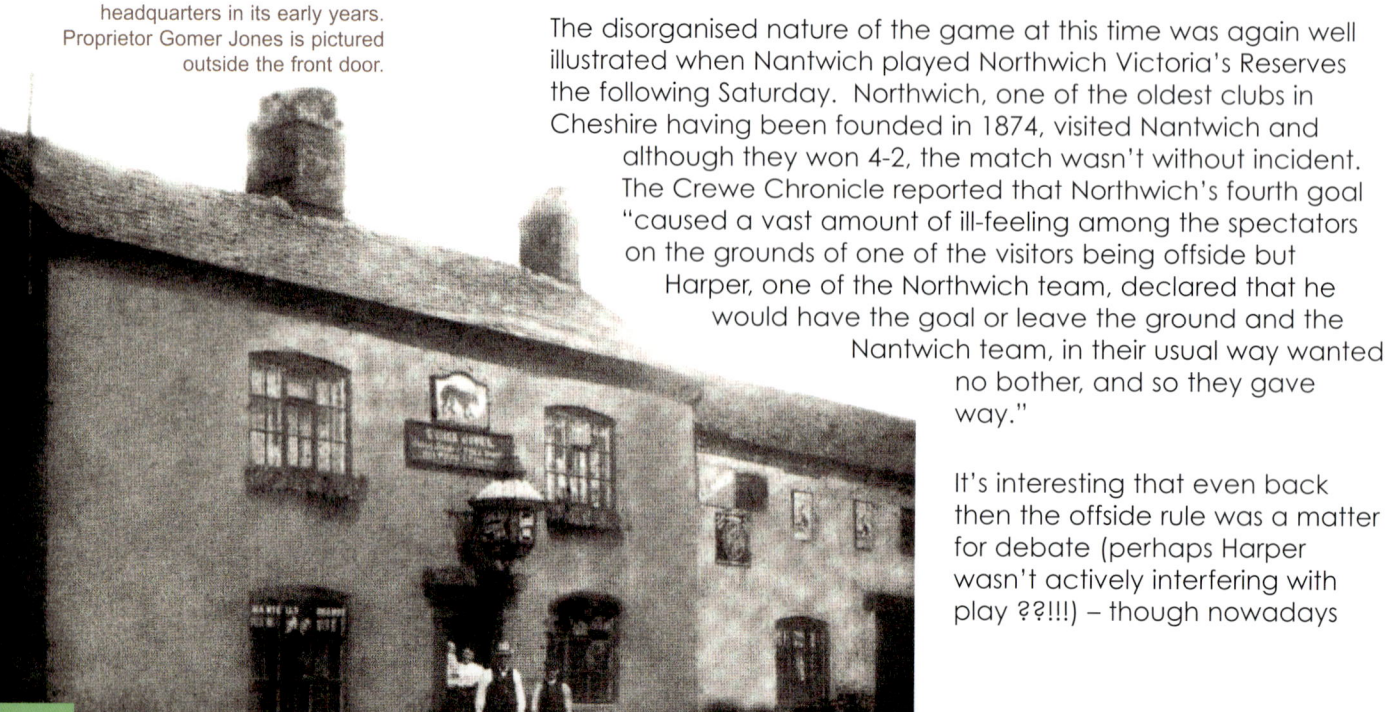

The disorganised nature of the game at this time was again well illustrated when Nantwich played Northwich Victoria's Reserves the following Saturday. Northwich, one of the oldest clubs in Cheshire having been founded in 1874, visited Nantwich and although they won 4-2, the match wasn't without incident. The Crewe Chronicle reported that Northwich's fourth goal "caused a vast amount of ill-feeling among the spectators on the grounds of one of the visitors being offside but Harper, one of the Northwich team, declared that he would have the goal or leave the ground and the Nantwich team, in their usual way wanted no bother, and so they gave way."

It's interesting that even back then the offside rule was a matter for debate (perhaps Harper wasn't actively interfering with play ??!!!) – though nowadays

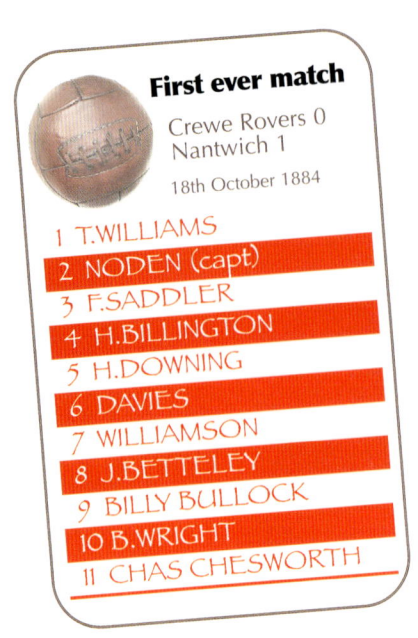

First ever match
Crewe Rovers 0
Nantwich 1
18th October 1884

1 T.WILLIAMS
2 NODEN (capt)
3 F.SADDLER
4 H.BILLINGTON
5 H.DOWNING
6 DAVIES
7 WILLIAMSON
8 J.BETTELEY
9 BILLY BULLOCK
10 B.WRIGHT
11 CHAS CHESWORTH

THE LEOPARD INN
The old Leopard Inn on London Road served as the club's headquarters in its early years. Proprietor Gomer Jones is pictured outside the front door.

IN THE BEGINNING

one suspects every team would happily prefer for an opponent to leave the ground than agree to give them a goal !

That match, on 1st November 1884, is believed to be the first played by the new Nantwich club at the old London Road ground. Back in 1884, there was little more than a field there and it soon fell into the ownership of Mr T Hitchin (subsequently a club Vice-President) and, in later years, to Gomer Jones – a local businessman who was licensee of the adjoining Leopard public house from 1891 to 1928 and who ran a drinks company there. In fact The Leopard effectively served as the club's headquarters for many years

In those days, friendly matches were the order of the day and the only competitive fixtures were cup matches. It was December 1884 before Nantwich took part in their first ever competitive match - a First Round tie in the Cheshire Senior Cup. The opponents that afternoon were Bollington White Star and Nantwich returned from Macclesfield having earned a hard-fought 4-3 victory.

There was more controversy in February 1885 when Nantwich played the return fixture against the Crewe Rovers club they had beaten in that first match. The game was goalless well into the second half when Hassall was sent clear for Nantwich. Lee, the Rovers' goalkeeper, claimed offside and made no attempt to stop Hassall's shot. Nantwich claimed a goal but Rovers (and some of the Nantwich players) insisted the ball should be thrown up at the spot where Hassall was offside. The Nantwich captain wouldn't agree to this so, as the Crewe Chronicle reported, "the Rovers left the ground amidst the shouting and hooting of the spectators."

The Nantwich team proved quite successful in its first season with impressive wins against Crewe Alexandra's 'A' team, Hanley Town, Middlewich and Chester St.Johns. Clearly, the club was here to stay and, as football continued to develop in Cheshire and across the country, the town of Nantwich was going to be part of that.

Players, of course, played the game for fun at that time - no wages or expenses. Just as well really as the club was hardly awash with money. In 1885 turnover for the whole year was just £27. It rose steadily over the next few years but financial concerns were to raise their head many times over the years.

In those dim and distant days of the late 1880s, clubs played relatively few games during a season. Cricket still took a major share of the nation's sporting calendar and it was unseemly for the football season to impinge on the well worn cricketing schedule. Football, then, hardly got going before mid-September and was rarely played after the middle of April.

During the late 1880s, Nantwich continued to play friendly games and compete in the Cheshire Senior Cup. In 1886/87, they were drawn to play Crewe Alexandra in the Third Round of the Cheshire

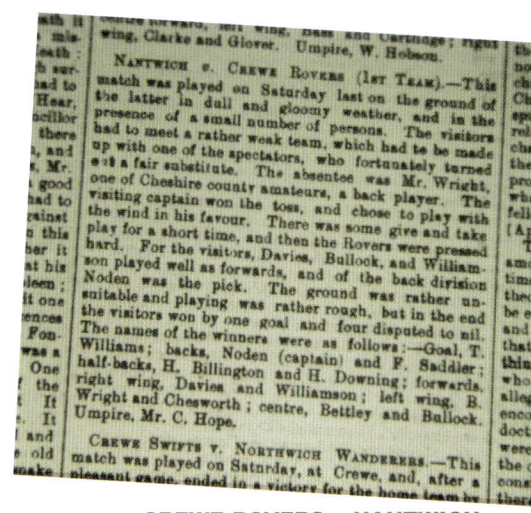

CREWE ROVERS v NANTWICH
18 October 1884
The first Nantwich match report in the Crewe Chronicle.

NANTWICH RESERVES 7
CREWE ROVERS RESERVES 0
18 October 1884
Nantwich Reserves' first game played on the same day as the first team's inaugural match. Line-up: H.Poole, Billington, H.Crawford, E.Crawford, Hollowood, Critchley, Barnett (capt), Bass, Cartlidge, Clarke, Glover. During this era it was customary to give reserve sides their own name. Nantwich's second string was referred to as Nantwich Swifts whilst Crewe Alexandra's second eleven were known as the 'Hornets' and Northwich Victoria also used the title 'Swifts' for their reserves.

IN THE BEGINNING

Turnover in the 1880s
- 1885 - £27
- 1886 - £68
- 1887 - £80
- 1888 - £92
- 1889 - £108

Cup. There was no more prestigious trophy than the Cheshire Cup at that time. Its popularity can be seen by the fact that a crowd of 5000 watched the 1886 final between Davenham and Crewe Alexandra at Middlewich whilst there was only 2000 at the Wales v England international at Wrexham that year.

Indeed, the tie against the Alexandra at the London Road ground attracted a crowd of 3000 but the match kicked off late. This was due to the visitors' bus breaking down just outside of Crewe so the Alex players had to walk the four miles to Nantwich. The Nantwich cause was aided by the famous Mr A.N. Hornby (see page 15) turning out for them. Hornby was known for his rugby and cricketing prowess and, as a resident of Nantwich, assisted the football and cricket clubs whenever he could. In some quarters he is credited with helping in the formation of the Crewe Alexandra club but, on this occasion, he helped the 'Saltmen' (as Nantwich were then nicknamed) to a 1-1 draw.

The replay was held at Crewe a week later. Another sizeable crowd of 3000 was in attendance, many of them holding up cards proclaiming 'Play up Alex' or 'Play up Nantwich' as was the custom in that era. This time, the Alex made their quality tell, winning by three goals to nil.

In 1888/89, Nantwich entered the FA Cup for the first time. The Cup, commonly known as the English Cup until the late 1920s, drew

click4more

All Nantwich's FA Cup results can be accessed at the on-line FA Cup archive. Visit: www.thefa.com/TheFACup/FACompetitions/TheFACup/Archive.aspx

NANTWICH FC SEASON TICKET 1888/89

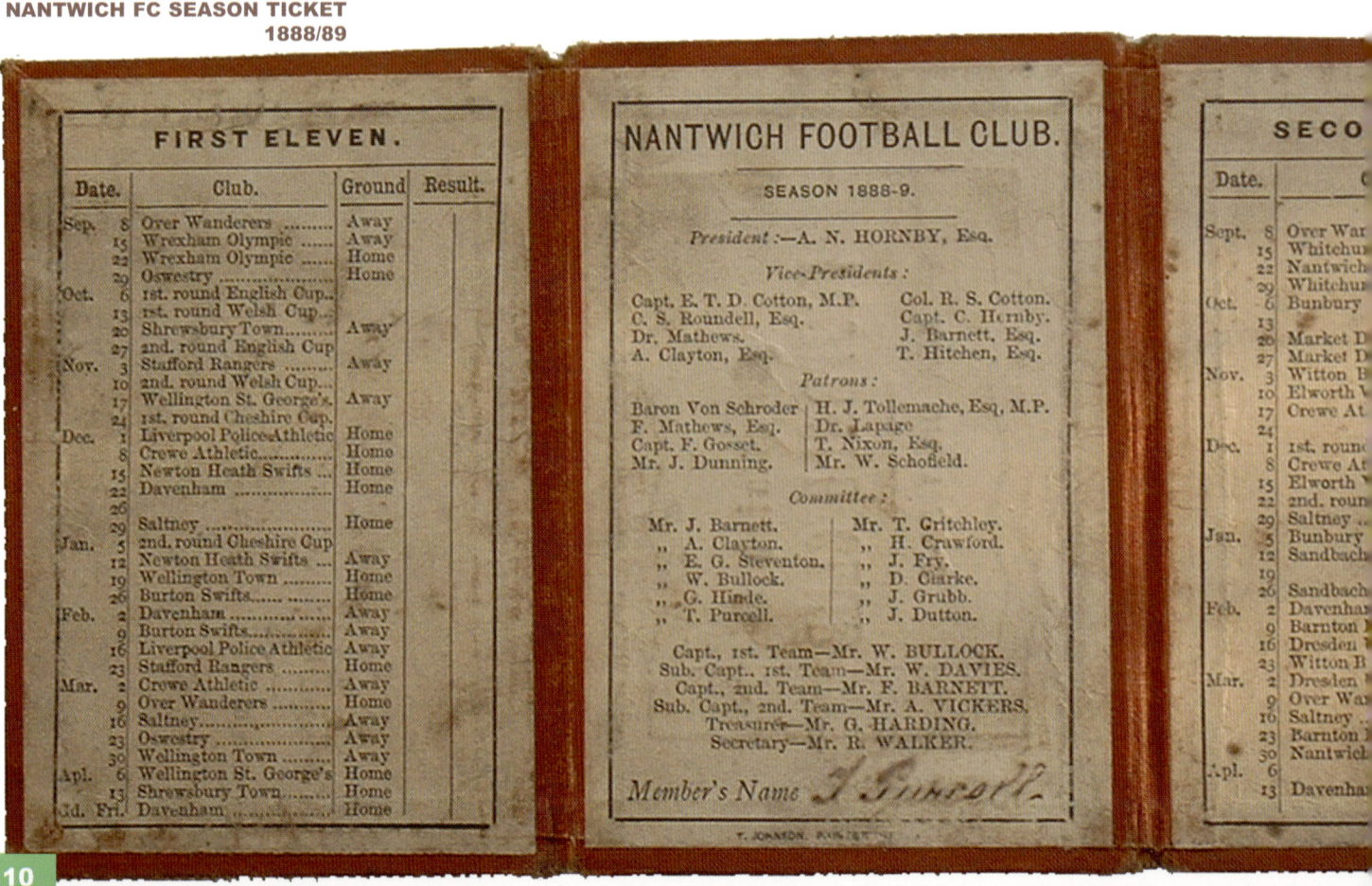

IN THE BEGINNING

entrants not just from England - but from Wales, Scotland and even Ireland. Nantwich played their first ever English Cup game away to Hartford St Johns on 6th October 1888 in the First Qualifying Round. Nantwich proved too strong for the Northwich side, easing to a 7-1 victory which set up a Second Qualifying Round tie away to Chirk. The Welsh border club were one of the strongest clubs of the time and they hammered a dozen goals past the Nantwich men without reply. To this day, that sorry scoreline remains Nantwich's heaviest FA Cup defeat.

Nantwich also entered the Welsh Cup for the first time that season. Drawn away to Crewe Alexandra in the First Round, the Alex scratched from the competition, giving Nantwich a free run into the Second Round. Another non-Welsh side were the opponents but after two 2-2 draws, Nantwich lost 5-1 to Davenham in a second replay.

The little club from the old market town was making fine progress, however. Just some six years after playing its first game, the club reached the final of the Cheshire Senior Cup. That 1889/90 season saw Nantwich knock out Davenham & Hartford United and Crewe Alexandra Hornets (both with 4-3 scorelines) to earn a coveted place in the final against Macclesfield.

The venue was switched from the traditional one at Middlewich to Northwich Victoria's Drill Field enclosure. Northwich were keen to promote the new venue and advertised in the top sports paper of the day - the 'Athletic News' - that they would give a £5 note to one person who correctly predicted the result of the game. We don't know who came to pocket the fiver but the promo must have helped as the match drew a crowd of 7000 paying receipts of £120 - then a record for the Final - with three special excursion trains having been laid on from the silk town.

Macclesfield were certainly taking the encounter seriously. Using the Queen's Hotel as their base, they went into special training. Alcohol and tobacco were banned and trainer John Allcock put his players under a regime of diet, country walks and Turkish baths in preparation for the big match.

For the game itself, Macclesfield looked resplendent in red, yellow and blue stripes but it was Nantwich who started colourfully, going ahead on 17 minutes. Bob Bull raced down the right and when his cross came over, Teddy Prince was on hand to head past Macclesfield goalkeeper Jack Kent. From there, it was

WALTER CARTWRIGHT

Born in Nantwich in January 1871, Cartwright played for his hometown side for two seasons in 1889/90 and 1890/91 and was selected to play for Cheshire - a great honour at the time. In his first season he helped Nantwich to a Cheshire Senior Cup Final clash with Macclesfield. He joined Heywood Central of the Lancashire League as a professional for the 1891/92 season. A diminiutive 5'8", Cartwright returned to Nantwich in September 1892 for the club's inaugural season in The Combination and was in the line-up for the FA Cup tie against Liverpool that season. Joining Crewe Alexandra in July 1893, utility man Cartwright made 50 League appearances for the Alex over the next two seasons in the Second Division before signing, in June 1895, for Manchester United – or Newton Heath as they were then known. Ironically he made his debut for the 'Heathens' against the Alex in the 5-0 victory in the Second Division on 7th September 1895. Cartwright, wearing Newton Heath's green and gold, scored twice in the 5-1 victory over Arsenal that season.

Newton Heath changed their name to Manchester United in 1902 and Cartwright, who weighed in at 10st 11lbs, played in the first League game for the club under its new name and in its new strip. The match in September 1902 (a 1-0 win at Gainsborough Trinity in the Second Division) saw United wear their famous colours of red shirts and white shorts for the first time.

Cartwright was the mainstay of United during this era – something of a Ryan Giggs of the late Victorian era. He played in every position, including in goal, and amassed 257 appearances in an era when the league season consisted of just 30 or 34 matches. The Nantwich man also scored 10 goals for United in a spell with the club lasting from 1895 until his retirement in 1905. In the tradition of former footballers, he later became a publican in Manchester. He died in 1930.

IN THE BEGINNING

1890 Cheshire Senior Cup Final
Macclesfield 4
Nantwich 1
22nd March 1890 at Northwich
Attendance: 5000   Receipts: £120

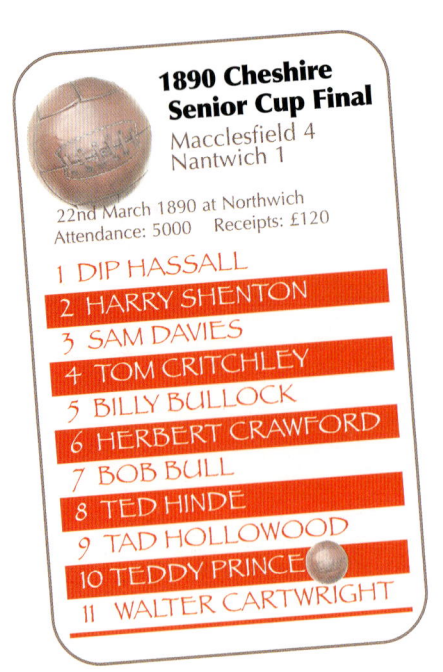

1 DIP HASSALL
2 HARRY SHENTON
3 SAM DAVIES
4 TOM CRITCHLEY
5 BILLY BULLOCK
6 HERBERT CRAWFORD
7 BOB BULL
8 TED HINDE
9 TAD HOLLOWOOD
10 TEDDY PRINCE
11 WALTER CARTWRIGHT

click4more

Nantwich's first ever game in a league competition was a home match against Newport in the Shropshire & District League on 12 September 1891. Nantwich led 2-0 at half-time and, at the final whistle, ran out 4-1 victors over their Shropshire visitors. Nantwich's league record season-by-season up to 1973 can be viewed at the Football Club History Database.
Visit:
www.fchd.info/NANTWICH.HTM

ALBERT HOLLOWOOD

'Tad' Hollowood, a renowned local cricketer, was the first man to score a hat-trick for Nantwich in a league match. He netted his treble in a 7-0 home win against local rivals Whitchurch in the Shropshire & District League on 26 September 1891.

sadly all downhill and, just before half-time, Nantwich keeper 'Dip' Hassall fisted the ball into the path of 'Mush' Howarth who volleyed home the equaliser. After the break, Macc's pre-match preparations started to tell and Nantwich came under the cosh for long periods - "Kent may have taken forty winks", one reporter drily commented. Two goals from Hindley and a long range punt from Tommy Lea condemned Nantwich to a 4-1 defeat - but they were far from disgraced. Although heavily beaten, Nantwich had competed well. Professionalism had begun to creep into football but, unlike 'Macc', Nantwich was still an amateur club - and reputedly the best in the county.

The run in the Cheshire Cup was followed the next season by a lengthy run in the English (FA) Cup. The 1890/91 Cup campaign started with the visit of Linfield Athletic. It must have been something of a trek for the Irishmen to reach Nantwich from their ground at Ulsterville Avenue in Belfast. The visitors, though, were overwhelming favourites, their strength evident by the fact that they went on to complete the Irish League and Cup double by the end of that season. 2000 spectators crammed into the ground and saw the local amateurs put up stiff opposition with Tad Hollowood netting the opening goal of the game. The Irishmen hit back to take a 2-1 lead but, in a game of fluctuating fortunes, Nantwich were back in the lead by half-time. The game turned again and with less than 10 minutes left on the clock, Linfield were holding a 4-3 lead. A Nantwich equaliser from a free-kick set up a tense finale. Then, with just two minutes remaining, Ted Hinde broke away to score the decisive goal in a thrilling 5-4 victory for the home side.

In the Second Qualifying Round, Nantwich secured a 3-2 win at Wrexham which set up another tense encounter in the Third Qualifying Round when Chester were the visitors. The Cestrians edged the tie 5-4 but such was the excitement that Mr Ormerod, the referee, had miscounted the goals and believed that Chester's late winner had only levelled the scores. Confusion reigned and with the referee preparing to play extra time, a small portion of the crowd surged onto the pitch, making for the Chester players. The Nantwich players and committee men tried to repel them and eventually, when order was restored, the referee confirmed Chester's narrow victory. Sadly, though, this was the first of a series of crowd misdemeanours that plagued Nantwich during those early years.

Friendlies and cup matches were the only games that Nantwich played at that time. The Football League had been formed in 1888 consisting of a single division of just 12 clubs. The new Football League did, however, act as a catalyst for more league competitions to be set up and, over the next few years, a sprinkling of leagues sprung up across the country.

Amongst those was the old Shropshire & District League which Nantwich joined in 1891. The league had actually been founded the previous season and included the likes of Shrewsbury Town, Stafford

IN THE BEGINNING

Rangers and Wellington Town. Nantwich soon proved themselves a force to be reckoned with - so much so that a letter appeared in the Crewe Chronicle in November from 'A Grieved Ratepayer'. He complained about youngsters playing football in streets in the town just because "the Nantwichians having won a few matches this season are quite elated with their success." !

In March, a 2-2 draw against reigning champions Ironbridge saw Nantwich in second place in the table and the following month, they were still in the hunt for the title when Wolverhampton Wanderers Reserves came to town. The Wolves side was top of the table and they proved too strong for Nantwich, securing a 3-0 victory in front of a crowd of 800. Wolves went on to clinch the title whilst Nantwich had to be content with the runners-up spot - a very creditable performance nonetheless.

SHREWSBURY TOWN v NANTWICH 5 October 1889
Shrewsbury Town's printed sheet advertising their FA Cup tie at home to Nantwich. These sheets also served as the matchday programme. Shrewsbury won this First Qualifying Round tie 3-2 but the match was ordered to be replayed as the Shrews fielded three ineligible players. Nantwich, though, sportingly scratched from the competition - giving Shrewsbury a walkover into the next round.

FOOTBALL MATCH.
ENGLISH CUP TIE.

SATURDAY, OCTOBER 5th, 1889.

Nantwich v. Shrewsbury Town.

ON

AMBLER'S FIELD,
ENTRANCE OPPOSITE RACECOURSE GRAND-STAND.

NANTWICH.

W. Hassall. (GOAL.)
S. Davies.   H. Shenton.
T. Critchley.   W. Buckley.
W. Cartwright.   H. Buckley.   H. Crawford.
E. Hind.
R. Bull.   E. Prince.
G. Rowlands.   A. Davies.   P. Murphy.
W. Morris.   A. Ellis.   H. Pearson. (Captain.)
L. Edwards.   J. C. Davies.
W. Steadman.   J. Jones.
(GOAL.)
J. Holbrook.

SHREWSBURY TOWN.

KICK-OFF AT 3-30 P.M.

ADMISSION **3d.**; Reserved Enclosure (Boarded Floor) **6d.**
REFRESHMENTS ON THE GROUND.

W. B. WALKER, (LATE BUNNY & DAVIES,) PRINTER, SHREWSBURY.

IN THE BEGINNING

NANTWICH 0 LIVERPOOL 4
15 October 1892
FA Cup 1st Qualifying Round

Liverpool FC was founded after a rent dispute between Everton FC and John Houlding who held the lease on the ground at Anfield. Houlding purchased Anfield in 1891, proposing an increase in the rent from £100 to £250 per year. Everton, who had been playing at Anfield for seven years, refused to meet his demands and moved to a new stadium in Goodison Park. Liverpool FC was then founded by Houlding on 15 March 1892 to play at the vacated Anfield. The original name was to be Everton Athletic, but when the FA failed to sanction the name, it was changed to Liverpool. This was Liverpool's first ever match in the FA Cup.

The success encouraged Nantwich to step up to The Combination for the 1892/93 campaign. It was a competitive league and saw Nantwich pitting their wits against some of the strongest sides in the region, including Chester, Wrexham, Stockport County as well as the reserve sides of Everton and Stoke. Perhaps it wasn't surprising that Nantwich should finish the season next to bottom of the table, just a point above Gorton Villa.

That same season, the English Cup threw up another intriguing tie for Nantwich. A new football club had been formed in the city of Liverpool after a dispute over rent at Everton's ground at Anfield (yes - would you believe the famous stadium used to be the home of the blue half of the city?!!)

Liverpool FC may have graced European stadia such as the San Siro and the Nou Camp and they may have won the coveted FA Cup seven times in their history but their first ever match in the world's oldest cup competition was played at Nantwich's humble London Road ground. The new Liverpool club went on to win the Lancashire League title in that inaugural season, having assembled a squad strong enough to beat the best. Most of the Liverpool players were 'foreigners' brought down from Scotland by the lure of attractive wages. Those who took the field at Nantwich included three Scottish internationals. In the circumstances, Nantwich did well to hold the Merseysiders goalless until 20 minutes from time. But then the heavy conditions took their toll on the home side (the match was played in a vile deluge) and their burly visitors pressed home their advantage, securing a 4-0 victory thanks to a hat-trick from John Miller and a strike by Tom Wylie.

The second season in The Combination was to prove something of a disaster. With just one league win all season, Nantwich finished bottom of the table. Moreover, financial clouds were gathering. The shift from being an amateur club to a professional one (or what would now be called semi-professional) had caused a strain on the finances and the increased travelling in The Combination was also taking its toll.

LIVERPOOL 1892/93
Back Row: J.McQue, J.McCartney, A.Hannah, S.Ross, M.McQueen, D.McLean, J.McBride, Mr.Dick (Trn).
Front Row: T.Wyllie, J.Smith, J.Miller, M.McVean, H.McQueen.

VICTORIAN SUPERSTAR

For a sporting superstar of Victorian times, you need look no further than Albert Neilson Hornby.

A.N. Hornby, as he was known, is one of only two men who have captained England at both rugby and cricket, topping the national batting averages in 1881. He won nine international caps at rugby between 1877 and 1882 and played in three cricket test matches from 1879 to 1884 at a time when sport at international level was played much less frequently than nowadays. Hornby was captain when England lost the Test match at home against the Australians in 1882, infamously giving rise to the series being dubbed 'The Ashes'.

Despite captaining Lancashire County Cricket Club into his 50s (he also later became its Chairman and President), he turned out for both Nantwich football and cricket clubs when time permitted after his family moved to Shrewbridge Hall from his native Blackburn.

Indeed such was his interest in local sport that he became President of Nantwich Cricket Club and served the football club in the same capacity for some twenty years from 1887 before William Travers Pickmere took over the role.

Nicknamed 'Monkey' or 'Boss', his appearance for Nantwich against Crewe Alexandra in the Cheshire Senior Cup in 1886 drew a crowd of 3000. It was reported that, as well as cricket and rugby, he could have played football at the highest level as he played a number of games for Blackburn Rovers, including their famous opening game at Alexander Meadows against Partick, the New Year game of 1878.

To round off his sporting CV, Hornby was on the Committee of the Rugby Football Union in the mid 1880s, was associated with the MCC from 1873 to 1898 and refereed major rugby matches after he retired from playing.

He married Ada Sarah Ingram in 1876, and they resided at Bridge House in Church Minshull, later at Poole Hall just outside Nantwich and then at Parkfield. His death brought much sorrow and he was laid to rest at Acton Church where his distinctive tombstone, showing wickets and a cricket bat, pays tribute to his sporting life. Hornby Drive in Nantwich was named in honour of this early sporting superstar.

A.N. HORNBY
Born Blackburn 10 February 1847
Died Nantwich 17 December 1925

THE LONDON ROAD GROUND

For over 120 years, Nantwich's old ground at Jackson Avenue provided the club and its supporters with a comfortable home. The ground, of course, pre-dated the road that is Jackson Avenue and, for much of its existence, was known as the London Road ground – being accessed by a pathway from off London Road. The pathway, subsequently, became Jackson Avenue when Jacksons the Builders constructed houses there in the post-war era.

Changing Rooms

Over the years, there had been a small array of buildings (some makeshift and some more permanent) at Jackson Avenue. Before changing rooms were built, the players changed in rooms at the back of the old Leopard Inn on London Road.

Before the end of the 19th century, the dressing rooms there were 6 yards long and 4 yards wide, well seated and with pegs. One was upstairs, the other downstairs. A bathroom was also available.

The configuration of the dressing rooms seems to have been altered before the First World War. Author Sid Simpson, recalls in his book 'Within Living Memory':

"(The Football Club) had their ground at the rear of the Leopard Inn … This area was, in earlier years, an open field with a path from Inn to ground. Mr Gomer Jones was the Innkeeper and proprietor of the Mineral Works alongside. A large entry divided the two buildings with a spacious room above both entry and works. Here were the dressing rooms for both home and visiting players, a wooden partition separating the teams at the rear. A door at each end was reached by an open stairway. So, spare a thought for the players of both teams as they ran the gauntlet of about 80 yards along the path before and after the game! The vociferous cheers, or at times jeers, that met them along the pathway was in itself a test of nerves. Boys and youths, of course, revelled in it – and woe betide the visitors should they have the audacity to beat the home side!"

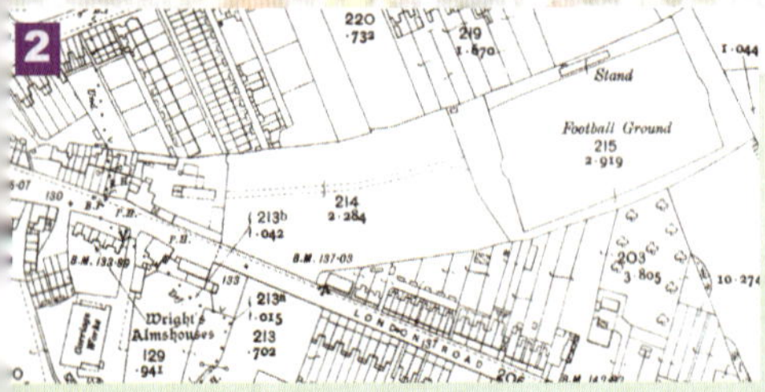

Perhaps it was just as well that dressing rooms were eventually constructed on the ground.

These were erected at the top left hand corner of the ground - a wooden hut painted in black and white stripes. And they were hardly salubrious ! So small, in fact, that sometimes some of the players changed outside. Hot water was a bit of a hit-and-miss affair, too, being heated by a coal boiler situated at the back. The boiler was lit several times on a Saturday morning to heat the water for the afternoon games. Often the boiler went out, though, so players had to wash in cold water. Needless to say that didn't go down well on a freezing winter's day.

At least the players had water in their dressing room. There was no water in the referee's changing hut which was situated alongside. The poor match official had to beg for water from the players - and you can imagine the response he got if he'd made a dodgy offside decision ! The old wooden dressing rooms served the club well.

Then in 1959, the Committee approved a 'ground improvement' scheme for new dressing rooms, grandstand, covered turnstiles and trainers boxes. First to go were the old dressing rooms, to be replaced by another wooden pavilion at the London Road end where the Social Club later stood. A matching pavilion stood in line with these dressing rooms across the main entrance and housed the canteen, kitchen and (rather small) Secretary's office. Before then, a solitary tea hut had stood at this bottom end of the ground.

Making a Stand

The first grandstand was built at the ground in 1896 at a cost of £50 (though it wasn't finally paid off until 1903) and was later sold off to Nantwich Cricket Club. Terracing was later introduced on the 'popular' side of the ground opposite. Admission to the ground in 1900 was 3d Adults and 1d for Children.

For many years, the playing pitch had a slope from top to bottom of some six feet - this being levelled out in the early sixties. With the step up to the Cheshire League in the late sixties, consideration was given to installing floodlights - but with a quote of £3600, the club couldn't afford them.

However, in the early 1970s, a replacement grandstand was constructed at a cost of over £5000. The old stand had been able to seat about 200 and when demolished, a hoard of old pop bottles were discovered underneath! These had evidently been discarded from Gomer Jones' old drinks factory, many still having the glass marble intact in the bottle neck.

Like its predecessor, the stand was situated central to the half-way line on the Crewe Road side of the ground. It provided seating for 165 spectators and helped the ground attain a 'C' grading in the mid 70s.

The space under the new grandstand was eventually converted into the dressing rooms. Worked started in 1981 but it was only after a £3000 grant had been secured from the Football Trust that the work was completed. The new dressing rooms were finally ready for the 1987/88 season, giving the ground a 'B' grading - the highest that could be achieved without installing floodlights. With the old dressing room pavilion now redundant, planning permission was obtained to replace them with a bar and canteen. The new Social Club was officially opened by Chairman-Secretary Jack Lindop on 14th September 1989.

---

1 - London Road at the end of the 19th century looking towards town. On the right is the old Leopard Inn. **2** - Early 20th century map showing the ground with the pathway leading to it from the changing rooms at the back of The Leopard. **3** - The changing rooms at the top of the ground pictured in 1959. **4** - The old stand, replaced in the early 70s.

IN THE BEGINNING

In the circumstances, Secretary Levi Jervis resigned (to be replaced by the safe hands of Billy Bullock and then William Chesworth). A sub-committee comprising John Williams, Thomas Hollinshead, Joseph Clarke, Billy Bullock and R.E.Walker was set up to examine the ailing financial position. They reported back that Jervis had paid the players greater expenses than the Committee had authorised. They requested that Mr Jervis should pay back the club the princely sum of £16 5s 6d - and he eventually consented to do so.

Unable to sustain a team in The Combination, Nantwich reverted to amateur status and dropped out of senior football. With the club reaching its 10th anniversary, The Cheshire Junior League was entered in 1894/95. Of course, as a 'junior' club Nantwich were not eligible to enter the English Cup or the Cheshire Senior Cup. Perhaps it was just as well - the previous season they had crashed 12-0 at Northwich Victoria in the First Round of the Cheshire Cup. 'Vics' were at the height of their power, rubbing shoulders with Arsenal, Liverpool and Manchester City in the Football League Second Division. Football legend Billy Meredith was learning his trade with the Vics and the Welshman netted twice in the humiliation of Nantwich that November afternoon.

Although membership of the Cheshire Junior League reduced travelling costs, further savings were needed and so the club dropped down to the Crewe & District Junior League for the 1895/96 campaign.

'The Wychers' racked up some hefty scorelines against what was obviously much weaker opposition. None so more than in April 1896 when Meadow Bank Swifts visited the London Road enclosure and were crushed 13-0.

The Cheshire Junior Cup was the forerunner to the Cheshire Amateur Cup and Nantwich progressed to the Semi-Finals where they embarked on a controversial tie at Knutsford. After the first match was drawn 2-2, Knutsford were overwhelmed 11-1 in the replay at Nantwich. However, the visitors claimed that the pitch was unfit and that the crossbar exceeded the permitted limit of 5 inches. The seemingly spurious appeal was upheld and the game was ordered to be replayed. This time Nantwich won 6-0 and, without any protests, marched through to the Final against Winnington Park Recreation.

Hosted at the Drill Field, Northwich, it proved to be a turbulent match with Edwards, the Winnington centre-forward being sent off. Although Nantwich won the game 3-2, the Cup wasn't presented after the match as Winnington had lodged a protest that the pitch was unplayable. For good measure, Nantwich themselves had put in a protest about the width of the crossbar - but this was withdrawn after the game! Sadly for Nantwich, the Cheshire FA again ruled that the pitch had indeed been unfit - despite the fact that it been passed as playable by the match referee Mr Collyer (who also happened to be the Secretary of the Crewe & District FA).

A STICKY MESS
Amazingly, Nantwich's heaviest home defeat was set way back in 1892. Everton Reserves were the visitors to the London Road ground on 3rd September - and they waltzed back to Merseyside with a 9-0 win under their belts. Perhaps it shouldn't have been too much of a surprise. The visitors were Combination champions and went on to retain their title at the end of the season. In fact, the Toffees' second string topped The Combination in seven out of eight seasons leading up to the turn of the century.

CHESHIRE FA CAP 1893/94
It was the pinnacle of a player's career to be selected for their County. Over the years a number of Nantwich players received this honour and this cap was awarded to John Garnett who was selected to play for Cheshire against Staffordshire on 30th September 1893. Played at the Drill Field, Northwich, the match ended in a 2-2 draw. Garnett went on to make a single League appearance for Northwich Victoria in the Second Division a couple of months later.

All final league tables of The Combination are available on-line. Visit:
www.rsssf.com/tablese/engcombinationhist.html

IN THE BEGINNING

NANTWICH FC - CHESHIRE JUNIOR CUP WINNERS 1896
Back Row (left to right): Bill Chesworth (Secretary), J.Wainwright, Harry Case, David Farrington, J.Farrington (Trainer).
Middle Row: Walter Case, T.Davies snr, Herbert Crawford,
Front Row: Will Edwards, Tom Davies jnr, W.Sutton, H.Williamson, Billy Betteley.

Having decided against taking legal action on the matter, Nantwich faced Winnington in the re-arranged game at Sandbach. A train was specially chartered to convey the enthusiastic Nantwich fans, about 800 in number, who helped to swell the attendance to 1800. After 15 minutes, the Northwich side took the lead and they held out until 10 minutes from time when an unruly element of the Nantwich support unsportingly tried to get the match abandoned. In the poetic words of the Crewe Chronicle, "the prospect of defeat loomed too ominously for some half drunken crowd of blackguards, who swept onto the field from behind the Winnington goal". One supporter headed straight for the referee, only to be tripped by a Winnington player and others from the crowd closed in to protect the referee. The flashpoint escalated and "blows were exchanged by at

IN THE BEGINNING

least a score of combatants". Eventually some order was restored but, unable to restart the game, the referee blew the final whistle and was escorted off the pitch to the dressing rooms. Realising that the mob had designs on grabbing the trophy, Mr Collyer (who had officiated in that first match) grabbed the cup and ran off into the town with it.

"Saturday's affair was a disgraceful business from beginning to end," summed up the Chronicle, "and everyone in Nantwich who is capable of thinking will be glad to forget it. We may add that there were half a dozen policemen on the ground and they were tossed about like corks in the ocean."

Mind you, if the aim of the marauders had been to get the match abandoned and replayed it certainly succeeded. It proved third time lucky and in a somewhat less eventful tussle, Nantwich held on to a slender 1-0 victory thanks to a goal from Davies. For the first time in the club's short history, Nantwich had won some silverware. There was jubilation in the town and some shops closed for a week as the town celebrated the football club's achievement.

Before the advent of Managers or Head Coaches, it was the trainer who got the best out of the players. Nantwich's trainer back then was J.Farrington, a former player who had been with the club in the first couple of seasons after being formed. The line up included two of the four Case brothers who all played for Nantwich - Harry, Walter, Tom and John. Tom, a goal getting centre forward, was perhaps the most successful of them and spent most of the first decade of the 20th century with Nantwich, interspersing his time at London Road with spells at Crewe Alexandra, Shrewsbury Town, Chester and Macclesfield. He was later to become landlord of the Union Vaults in Nantwich. The fifth brother, Edward, became a great football administrator. He served as President of the Cheshire FA and, in 1919, was honoured to be named the first President of the Cheshire County League which he served with great distinction until his death in 1952. Although born in Nantwich, Ted moved to West Kirby and also had a brief spell as a Director of Tranmere Rovers.

Thanks partly to the cup success, financial stability had been restored and at the 1896 AGM, Bill Chesworth, in his first season as secretary, was pleased to report that the club had cleared off its old debts of £8 and would start the 1896/97 season with funds in the bank.

A brave attempt was made to retain the Cheshire Junior Cup but having reached the Final again, opponents Barnton Albion proved too strong and the holders went down 3-1.

1896 Cheshire Junior Cup Final
Nantwich 1
Winnington Park Recreation 0
29th April 1896 at Chester   Att: 1000

1 HARRY CASE
2 J.WAINWRIGHT
3 DAVID FARRINGTON
4 WALTER CASE
5 T.DAVIES snr
6 HERBERT CRAWFORD
7 WILL EDWARDS
8 TOM DAVIES jnr
9 W.SUTTON
10 H.WILLIAMSON
11 BILLY BETTELEY

19

IN THE BEGINNING

1898 CHESHIRE SENIOR CUP FINAL
Nantwich 0
New Brighton Tower 1
16 April 1898 at Crewe

Nantwich: Dip Hassall, J.Wainwright, T.Davies, Kelly, D.Hall, Herbert Crawford, W.Sutton, Ted Howard, G.Betts, Sammy Barnett, Billy Betteley. Attendance: 5000
Nantwich were underdogs in the Final to opponents who had only been formed in 1897 and played at the cavernous Tower Athletic Grounds which boasted a capacity of 80,000. The owners of New Brighton tower, an Eiffel Tower style attraction built to rival Blackpool's, had developed the stadium next to the tower to provide winter entertainment. The club joined the powerful Lancashire League and after finishing as champions in their first season were elected to the Football League. There was quite a furore as a number of internationals were signed but despite success on the field, there was little enthusiasm for the club in the seaside resort with attendances only averaging around the 1000 mark. After three seasons in the Second Division, running costs proved too high and the short-lived club folded in 1901.

By the late 1890s, Nantwich had become something of a springboard for players to progress into the Football League which, at the time, still consisted of just two Divisions and included the likes of Northwich Victoria and Glossop North End. Herbert Birchenough, Walter Cartwright, Herbert Crawford and Billy Betteley were just a few of the pioneers of Nantwich football who made the grade in League football. They turned out to be the forerunners of over 50 players who, over the club's 125 years, have stepped up to play in the Football League after learning their trade with Nantwich.

Perhaps the best known at the time was Walter Cartwright (see page 11) who joined the famous 'Red Devils' before they played in red and before they were called Manchester United !!

It was felt that the time was right for a new challenge so, for the 1897/98 season, senior status was re-adopted and the Wychers stepped up to the North Staffordshire & District League. To boost the squad, Betts was signed from Coppenhall and Betteley returned after having spent the previous season with Congleton.

Eight years after reaching their first Cheshire Senior Cup final, Nantwich repeated the feat in 1898. Congleton Hornets, Barnton Albion and Chester were all defeated on the way to meeting the then mighty New Brighton Tower in the Final at Crewe. The seasiders had the England goalkeeper of the time Jack Robinson in goal. Robinson had played in all England's home internationals the month before - so Nantwich's forwards would have to be on their game to test him. It is probably the strongest side Nantwich have ever played against and boasted another four full internationals. 'The Towerites' full line-up was: Jack Robinson (England), Donald Gow (Scotland), Smart Arridge (Wales), Charlie McEleny, Geordie Dewar (Scotland), R.Ellison, Andrew Hamilton, Charlie Henderson, Harry Hammond, Tommy Tierney, Alf Milward (England).

New Brighton started the better but against the run of play Nantwich almost took the lead when Betts struck the crossbar. Nantwich held out to half-time and started to come more into the match after the interval but with just four minutes remaining, Hammond beat Dip Hassall in the Nantwich goal and Tower lifted the trophy.

Football matches at the time were also colourful affairs with teams playing in a rainbow of colours and clubs changing their colours every few seasons. Nantwich's early colours were scarlet and white stripes but it wasn't long before they gave way to blue and white stripes with blue shorts.

Despite success in other cup competitions, Nantwich had singularly failed to make an impact in the English Cup. That changed somewhat in the 1899/00 season when Winsford United and Warrington were put to the sword, giving the club a plum draw away to Burslem Port

'DIP' HASSALL'S MEDAL FROM THE 1898/99 CREWE & DISTRICT FA CUP FINAL
Nantwich beat Northwich Victoria 1-0 in front of a crowd of 4000 at Crewe.

NANTWICH'S 'GRAND OLD MAN OF FOOTBALL'

Revered as Nantwich's 'Grand Old Man of Football', William Chesworth had an enduring passion for Nantwich Football Club. Bill, as he was known, had been one of the club's earliest players shortly after its formation in 1884 and later went on to serve as Secretary for 11 years from 1895 and filled the breach again for the 1920/21 season. With his grasp of finances, it's not surprising that he also had a spell as club Treasurer. A resident of London Road (where else!) he was instrumental, with Mr L Vaughan, in procuring the first grandstand at the old ground in 1896.

Remarkably, Bill's daughter, Doris Hammersley, was the club's guest of honour at the final game played at the old London Road ground in 2007 - some 120 years after her father had first become involved with Nantwich Football Club. To continue the family association, Doris' son Kevin is a keen Nantwich supporter - and Kevin's sister, Jane, married Carl Betteley, a grandson of Billy Betteley who was a regular in the Nantwich line-up at the turn of the 20th century.

Mr Chesworth was a well known figure locally and would often be seen drawing on his faithful pipe. He worked for over 40 years at Heaps Clothing Factory in Nantwich before retiring at the grand age of 83 and was a life member of Nantwich Liberal Club. His service as a football administrator saw him join the Crewe & District FA in 1896, later being awarded a medal for 25 years' service. He was senior auditor for Cheshire FA over three decades, ill health forcing him to step down at the age of 86 - just one year before he passed away in 1955.

He was a keen supporter of Nantwich Cricket Club and donned the whites for the old Church House side for many a year in the summer. He was also a renowned bowls player - but his first love was always Nantwich FC. Shortly before his death, he recalled the most memorable match ever played by Nantwich as being the 1898 Cheshire Senior Cup Final. "It was against a New Brighton Tower side comprising a welter of full internationals," he reminisced. "They included Jack Robinson (formerly with Derby County), Donald Gow (Sunderland), Alf Milward (Everton) and Harry Hammond (Blackburn Rovers). There was no score until four minutes from time. From a foul, Hammond scored the winning goal."

And the best goal he saw in 70 years of watching the Dabbers? A strike from Ted Howard playing against an all-professional Congleton side in 1897/98. "Ted, at inside-right, got the ball in his own half and out-manoeuvred six opponents before beating Jack Kent with a grand shot." Finances, of course, had always been tight. A couple of years earlier he had proudly seen his side lift the Cheshire Junior Cup. "The receipts from the 3rd and 4th rounds were 1s 2d and 1s 4d, so we didn't make much out of that," he remembered.

Bill Chesworth relaxing on Blackpool sands with his wife in the 1920s.

Bill Chesworth's daughter Doris Hammersley receives, on behalf of the club, a watercolour of the old ground from artist Peter Greene (left) before the last game at Jackson Avenue, with Chairman Clive Jackson and President Michael Chatwin lending a hand.

IN THE BEGINNING

THOMAS DAVIES
Tom was part of Nantwich's 1896 Cheshire Junior Cup winning side before going on to join Burslem Port Vale in August 1899, making his League debut at left-back in a 5-0 defeat at Bolton Wanderers on 2nd January 1900. He was a regular from September 1900 until 1902 but was released at the end of the 1902/03 season, later returning to London Road.

Vale in the Third Qualifying Round. The Vale, then standing fifth in the Second Division, were not exempt from the latter qualifying rounds as League clubs are today but the visit of the men from the salt town failed to capture the imagination. The counter attraction at Stoke, who were at home to Everton, kept the crowd down to a measly 600 on a blustery afternoon. Nantwich did well to match their League opponents but after 25 minutes right back Wainwright had to hobble off with an injury. The Vale took full advantage and Scotsman Jimmy Reid put the home side ahead. Nantwich were desperately unlucky not to level matters when Mort and Will Edwards struck the bar in quick succession but stalwart Billy Heames added a late second goal to give the scoreline some respectability for the Valiants. "Nantwich were deservedly complimented on their fine performance against such strong opposition," remarked the Crewe Guardian.

By the turn of the century, there had been no major increase in Nantwich's population as neighbouring Crewe continued to expand. The town, noted for the number of buildings which had survived from the sixteenth and seventeenth century, was starting to look a bit shabby in places as some of the timber-framed cottages fell into disrepair. A degree of 'slum' clearance took place to help smarten up the town and motor cars were to be seen on a more regular basis, beetling around the town's streets.

In January 1901, Queen Victoria passed away, so bringing to an end a reign of over 63 years. For the country, it was a time of change and so it proved to be for Nantwich Football Club as well. After three seasons in the North Staffordshire & District League, the club had a solitary season in the old short-lived Cheshire League (not to be confused with the Cheshire County League which started up in 1919) before stepping back up to the 'big time' with re-joining The Combination.

NANTWICH RESERVES 1901/02

That 1900/01 season had seen Nantwich pipped to the Cheshire League title by Burslem Port Vale Reserves. Ironically, if the Wychers (as the club was still nicknamed) hadn't had two points deducted for playing an ineligible player, they would have scooped their first league title. Even so, the club could have lifted the crown had they secured a point against the Vale Reserves in the defining last match of the campaign. 2-0 up, the title looked there for the taking but Nantwich caved in conceding three second half goals to throw away the match - and the championship.

Disappointment and frustration got the better of the Nantwich faithful and, in unruly scenes, the crowd swarmed onto the pitch with three minutes remaining. They were angry with the decisions of the referee - a stand-in official as the league, evidently, had not appointed a referee for the match! Police supervision prevented the mob from dishing out any retribution on the stand-in and if their aim was to get the match abandoned, it succeeded. However, the result was ruled to stand

IN THE BEGINNING

and Nantwich Football Club was censured in the strongest terms. Costs of a commission to look into the affair had to be borne by the club which was ordered to post Football Association warnings around the ground - and ensure that future games were properly policed.

More drama came in the English Cup with the club reaching the Fifth Qualifying Round of the competition. The Cup was organised differently from how it is nowadays. For a start, the Football League only operated a First and a Second Division – so only had some 36 clubs in its ranks. The Cup had five qualifying rounds and an 'Intermediate' Round before the First Round Proper. There were only three rounds before the Semi-Final, compared to the six rounds we now have. So, in actual fact, Nantwich were one of the last 52 clubs left in the competition!

Having won 3-0 at Middlewich Athletic Rangers in the First Qualifying Round, Nantwich were rewarded with another derby game, taking on Winsford United in the Second Qualifying Round.

WILLIAM BETTELEY

Born in Nantwich in 1876, Billy was a true stalwart who enjoyed a number of spells with his home-town club. He started playing for Nantwich Church House as a 15 year old before joining Nantwich in 1893 - playing outside left alongside Frank Chesworth. His goals helped Nantwich lift the Cheshire Junior Cup in 1895/96. Though he spent the following season with Congleton, he returning to London Road in the 1897 close season and featured in the side that lost 1-0 to New Brighton Tower in the 1898 Cheshire Cup Final. In the 1899/1900 season, he joined Glossop, then members of the First Division of the Football League, but was unable to gain a place in their side. He signed for Stockport County whom he served for three and a half years, winning the Manchester Cup and Lancashire League. He figured in Stockport's first ever League match on 1st September 1900, and was on the scoresheet as County drew 2-2 at Leicester Fossee in a Second Division fixture. Also in County's line-up that day was W.J. (Joe) Forster who later played for Nantwich with his brother, Jack. Betteley netted six times for County in 44 League appearances over that and the following season. He spent the 1903/04 season with Crewe Alexandra, scoring 5 times in 24 appearances in the Birmingham & District League. He re-joined Nantwich in the 1904/5 season and left for Stafford Rangers during the 1907/08 campaign. He moved on to Stafford Albion in December 1907 but later returned to Nantwich, playing up to the outbreak of the Great War with the exception of the bulk of the 1909/10 season, spent at Whitchurch. Making sure he maintained a high level of fitness enabled him to continue playing for Nantwich to the age of 38, earning a benefit match against Stoke on 2nd April 1915 – some 22 years after first turning out for the club. Sadly, he lost his life on 4th April 1917 during service in the First World War and lies in Arras cemetery in France.

'The Cobblers', as Nantwich were also known in reference to the town's shoe-making industry, defeated their neighbours 5-2 to earn another home tie in the Third Qualifying Round. Nantwich were again victorious, a late goal from Lowrie helping to beat Buxton 2-1 and setting up a date at Earlestown in the Fourth Qualifying Round. Nantwich's opponents were then members of the strong Lancashire League, yet the visitors still won through with a superb 3-2 victory.

This gave Nantwich a dream tie at neighbours Crewe Alexandra in the Fifth Qualifying Round. The Alex were also members of the Lancashire League and had England international Len Hales in their line-up. The pitch was slightly the worse for wear and so had been heavily sanded. A crowd of 5000 watched the Gresty Road clash and saw the home side take control of the game. There was to be no giant-killing and, by half-time, Crewe were 4-0 up. The second half was a more even affair but despite a late consolation goal from Lowrie, Nantwich went down by a 5-1 scoreline.

There was another good Cup run the following season. Wins against Winsford United and Birkenhead secured a home tie against Second

IN THE BEGINNING

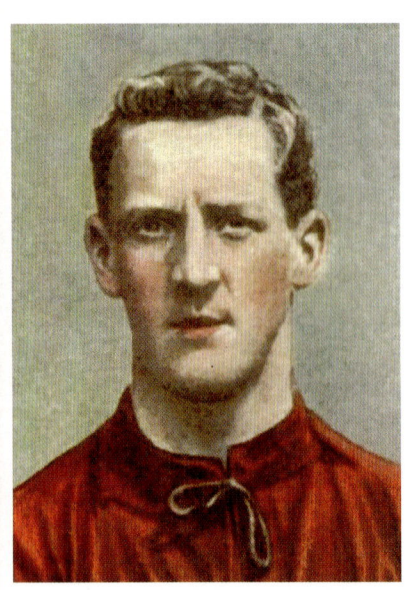

ARTHUR GODDARD
Glossop's 'Flyer' terrorised the home defence in the Cup tie played at Nantwich on 16th November 1901. He later played for Liverpool, as pictured here, scoring 75 goals in 388 League appearances.

Division Glossop in the Fourth Qualifying Round. The Hillmen had former Nantwich keeper Herbert Birchenough in goal and two celebrated players in their ranks: Johnny Goodall and Arthur Goddard. Goodall had been capped 14 times by England and was a member of the exclusive band of players who played in the first ever set of Football League fixtures back on 8th September 1888. That season, he was leading scorer for Preston North End in the "Invincibles" Double-winning side that lifted the League title without losing a match. His strike partner Goddard was nicknamed 'the Flyer' for his devastating pace down the flanks and before long he'd be playing regular First Division football with Liverpool and gain selection for the Football League representative team.

The conditions weren't great for football - a frost-bound pitch and fog as thick as pea soup. The League side settled the faster and took an early lead when Scotsman George Badenoch lifted the ball into the net. Nantwich were still struggling with the slippy surface and Astbury headed into his own goal to give Glossop a second. Although Arthur Davies pulled a goal back, 'the Flyer' wrapped it up rushing down the right wing at the speed of an express train before banging the ball into the net.

Nantwich had clearly been bitten by the English Cup bug and, after finishing runners up in The Combination the previous season, the Wychers enjoyed another epic Cup run in 1903/04. The odyssey had begun in quiet fashion that season - a bye in the First Qualifying Round. Then, a first-half goal from Arthur Davies secured a 1-0 victory over Middlewich Athletic Rangers, setting up a Third Qualifying Round tie with St.Helens Recreation. The sides were closely matched and after a 1-1 draw at the old London Road ground, Nantwich overcame their Lancashire Combination opponents 3-2 in the replay. A Tommy Astles penalty and two goals from Arthur Davies saw the Cobblers win through after extra time.

The Fourth Qualifying Round saw a trip to Stalybridge Rovers – forerunners of present day Stalybridge Celtic. Goals from Tom Case and another Tommy Astles spot-kick gave Nantwich a 2-1 half-time lead. Despite second-half pressure from the Lancashire Combination side, Nantwich held on to secure a home tie with Burslem Port Vale in the Fifth Qualifying Round on 28th November 1903.

There is little doubt that the game was one of the biggest in Nantwich's long history. The Vale were in Division Two at the time but Nantwich were looking for revenge for that Cup defeat by Vale four years earlier. This time, the tie was at Nantwich and 2000 spectators crammed into the ground, paying a total of £32 in gate receipts.

Nantwich took the game to the Vale and Harry Cotton, the former Nantwich keeper, was called on to tip a shot over the bar. Despite the pressure, Nantwich struggled to break the deadlock and after the interval Rol White should have put the Wychers ahead as could reserve striker G.H.Smith, standing in for the prolific Lowrie.

HERBERT BIRCHENOUGH

Not many footballers have gone on to feature for Manchester United after playing for Nantwich – but goalkeeper Herbert Birchenough is one. He spent a season with the Wychers before moving into League football with Port Vale, Glossop (then in the League) and, yes, Manchester United. His prowess between the sticks was such that he gained representative honours - being selected to play for the Football League.

Born in Haslington in 1874, Birchenough started out with Haslington Villa and joined Crewe Alexandra as a teenager, playing for their reserve eleven – 'the Hornets'. Nantwich, at the time, were playing in The Combination – and were in desperate need of a decent keeper. The defence had shipped 80 goals in 22 league games during the 1892/93 season, finishing next to bottom, and Birchenough was seen as the ideal man to stem the flood of goals.

The promising youngster joined for the start of the new campaign but sadly, his presence did little to help. Nantwich continued to struggle (including a 12-0 mauling at Northwich Victoria in the Cheshire Senior Cup) and the young goalkeeper moved on to Sandbach St Mary's and Audley before signing for Burslem Port Vale (as they were then known) in October 1897.

He helped the Valeites, who were then a non-league club, to a shock victory over Sheffield United in the 1897/98 FA Cup competition – the Blades going on to become League champions that season.

The upset helped Vale to get elected to the Football League the following season. Birchenough proudly took his place in goal for Vale's inaugural League match at home to Barnsley on 3rd September 1898. Vale won 3-0 and, in a fantastic start to League life, Birchenough kept five clean sheets in Vale's first six League matches which they all won. Sadly, the Burslem side fell away as the season progressed - finishing ninth with Birchenough missing just one game.

The former Nantwich custodian made a further 18 League appearances for Vale the following season and his displays brought him to the attention of the Football League selection committee. He was chosen to play for the Football League against the Irish League at Burnden Park, home of Bolton Wanderers, in November 1899. Although he didn't keep a clean sheet, the Football League won 3-1.

Now 25, Birchenough was at the height of his career, making a step up to the top flight of the League when he was transferred to struggling Glossop North End at the end of January 1900. Alas, Birchenough could not turn around their fortunes and the Peak side finished bottom at the end of their one and only season in the First Division and were relegated back down to the Second.

The 1900/01 season saw Birchenough as an ever-present in the side as the Hillmen finished in a creditable 5th place in the Second Division. Then, in November 1901, Birchenough made an emotional return to Nantwich when his Glossop side was paired against his former club in the FA Cup. On the day, Nantwich proved no match for their illustrious visitors. Birchenough contributed to his former club's downfall, making a breathtaking save from Nantwich half-back Tommy Astles as Glossop notched up a 3-1 victory.

Birchenough's time at Glossop was drawing to a close and, although he made a single appearance at the start of the following campaign, he switched to Manchester United in October 1902. United at the time were also operating in the Second Division and were gearing up to reach their glories of later years. The former Nantwich keeper made his United debut at Woolwich Arsenal ensuring the Gunners only fired blanks in a 1-0 victory.

He went on to make 26 League appearances for United as they finished 5th that season - many of those appearances being alongside Walter Cartwright another former Nantwich player who went on to play for the Red Devils.

In May 1903, Birchenough moved on again – or moved back to be more precise. He signed on for Crewe Alexandra, ten years after originally leaving the Alex for Nantwich. Having lost their League status in 1896, Crewe were plying their trade in the strong Birmingham & District League and Birchenough went straight into the Crewe line-up for their opening game of the 1903/04 season.

For the next six seasons, the Haslington man was virtually an everpresent for the Alex, making his last appearance in a Cheshire Senior Cup semi-final tie against Witton Albion in March 1910,

Now turned 35, it was time for Birchenough to hang up his gloves on a distinguished career. He died in 1942. Herbert's son, Frank, would follow in his footsteps, becoming Nantwich's number one before sampling League football with Burnley and West Ham United just after the Great War.

THE LEAGUE MEN
Nantwich players who have gone on to feature in the Football League
Part 1: Before the First World War

Sammy Barnett (1892, Crewe 62 League appearances, 7 goals)
RH.Keay (1892, Crewe 1)
Walter Cartwright (1893, Crewe 50,1; Newton Heath/
   Manchester United 228,9)
Herbert Crawford (1893, Crewe 57)
John Garnett (1893, Northwich Victoria 1)
Sam Davies (1894, Bury 42,5; Luton 25,1)
George Batho (1895, Crewe 15)
Champion (1895, Crewe 1)
Herbert Birchenough (1898, Burslem Port Vale 51, Glossop 81,
   Manchester United 25
Tom Davies (1899, Burslem Port Vale 58)
Billy Betteley (1900, Stockport 44,6)
Frank Chesworth (1900, Glossop 28,6; Stockport 28,6)
Alfred Maybury (1900, Burslem Port Vale 32, Chesterfield 9)
Thomas Wainwright (1900, Burslem Port Vale 21,
   Notts County 8)
Harry Cotton (1901, Burslem Port Vale 124)
W Galley (1903, Glossop 11)
Billy Weaver (1907, Bolton 4,1)
Fred Condrey (1911, Nottm Forest 7,2)
Albert Ralphs (1911, Aston Villa 1)

IN THE BEGINNING

Vale then hit back with former Wolves striker Joseph Holyhead having a 30 yard drive held by Nantwich keeper Ike Barnes. Then with 20 minutes to go, the visitors went ahead. Debutant Dick Allman hit the bar and Adrian Capes, Vale's goal machine of that era, was on hand to knock in the rebound from close range. The Vale hung on to their slender 1-0 lead and went on to meet Southampton in the First Round Proper. It would be another 105 years before Nantwich reached the final qualifying round of the Cup again!

The 1903/04 side certainly proved to be one of the strongest in the club's history and included the likes of Tommy Astles, Frank Chesworth and Rol White. Known as 'Carey', Astles was deadly from free kicks and spot-kicks and his menacing long throws were a useful addition to the Wychers' armoury. Chesworth was in his second spell with the club. Nicknamed 'Thunder', it was said he could head the ball as far as most could kick it. He'd left Nantwich to play League football with Glossop and Stockport County and on his return was converted from a forward to a left back. At the end of the 1905/06 season he left London Road to join Stretford and later played for Witton Albion. Sadly he died in a tragic accident at the tender age of 32, falling from a tramcar in February 1907. White, also a forward, had played for the club at the turn of the century before moving on to Rhyl in 1901. He returned for the 1903/04 season and signed for Chester in the 1904 close season. He was known to be forever smiling and was reputed to be one of the best dribblers of the ball. Re-joining Nantwich for a third time a season later, he carried on playing for the club to the end of the decade, being made club captain in the process. White was also a cricketer in the North Staffordshire League with Crewe Alexandra CC and he sadly died in September 1920 at the age of 41.

It was perhaps no surprise that such a strong Nantwich team should reach the 1904 Final of the Cheshire Senior Cup. The match took place at the Drill Field and the opponents were Chester - who finished the season as runners-up in The Combination, just one place above Nantwich. Lowrie thumped home Jack Forster's cross to put Nantwich 1-0 up and then on the half-hour Rol White was bundled over by Poultney. Astles made no mistake with the penalty but the referee ordered it to be re-taken as he hadn't blown his whistle. Astles' usual precision deserted him on the re-take and it was fisted away by Bill Coventry, Chester's former Crewe keeper who would join Nantwich later in his career. It was a costly miss as Tommy Delaney equalised for Chester in the second half.

Nantwich A.F.C. 1903-4.

Photo by R. Scott & Co., Granville St., Manchester.
W. Chesworth   T. Astles   T. Davies   W. Garnett   J. Large   F. Chesworth   J. Billington, Trainer
W. Layton   A. Davies   T. Case   J. Barnes   R. White   F. Lowrie

1904 Cheshire Senior Cup Final replay
Chester 2
Nantwich 1 after extra time
23rd April 1904 at Crewe
Attendance: 5000   Receipts: £121 1s 6d

1 IKE BARNES
2 COX
3 W. DAVIES
4 HARRISON
5 WILL GARNETT
6 FRANK CHESWORTH
7 TOMMY ASTLES
8 ARTHUR DAVIES
9 JACK FORSTER
10 ROL WHITE
11 F. LOWRIE

27

IN THE BEGINNING

BILLY WEAVER

Born Shropshire, 5 November 1885. 5'8", 10st 7lbs. Played for Nantwich in 1903/04 before moving to Crewe Alexandra in December 1904 where he spent two seasons. An old fashioned right winger, he had a spell with Whitchurch in 1906/07, joining Bolton Wanderers later in the campaign. 'Wiley' as he was known, played four times for the Trotters, his debut goal giving them their first ever win at Sunderland. Uncle to Harry Boston, he returned to Nantwich from Wellington Town in October 1909. He continued playing up to and beyond World War One, taking on trainer responsibilities and later becoming a scout for Bolton.

A week later, the sides clashed again in the replay at Crewe. In trying to clear Tommy Lipsham's corner, Nantwich keeper Ike Barnes put through his own goal but Lowrie levelled matters and sent the game into extra time. Barnes, who later became a much-respected referee, got a nasty kick on the leg and although he carried on (there were no substitutes back then!), the injury stopped him getting to the Tommy Delaney shot that clinched an extra-time victory for the Cestrians.

Sadly, the achievements on the pitch were again marred by crowd behaviour off it. When the Reserves faced Coppenhall in the Crewe & District League, the referee reported that a spectator had struck him between the eyes and on the head. The unruly element had also flung bricks and clods at him as he left the ground. The Cheshire FA instructed the club to take proceedings against the offender on behalf of the referee.

The Nantwich public again had the chance to see international players on their home turf when Second Division Glossop returned to London Road for an English Cup clash in October 1904. As they had three years earlier, Glossop had an international by the name of Goodall in their line-up. This time it wasn't Johnny - but centre half Arthur, an Irish international but now turned 40. On the left wing, they also boasted former England international Fred Spiksley.

The Wychers put in a splendid performance but Glossop's experience eventually told and despite a Jack Forster goal, Nantwich lost 2-1

In 1905, the first open top omnibus service began between Nantwich and Crewe. Whether it was used to convey Nantwich fans to Crewe for what became traditional Good Friday clashes with the Alex reserves we do not know. Either way, in later years, many would forsake the bus - hundreds walking to the railway town with their bells and rattles in a noisy procession. The games generated huge interest and for those unable to make the short trip to Crewe, pigeons would convey the half-time score back to Nantwich. Likewise, the Alex would visit London Road for the return fixture on Easter Monday and the matches would invariably attract bumper crowds.

The gate receipts from the Crewe game would become very important to the cash-stricken Cobblers. The last four matches of

28

IN THE BEGINNING

the 1904/05 season had only brought in a total of £15 in gate receipts. Winsford United, in more severe financial straits, bowed out of The Combination because of their debts of £33 but Nantwich decided to soldier on in what was a very competitive league.

For the 1907/08 season, the club entered the Welsh Cup for the first time since the early 1890s when they'd been in the habit of withdrawing from the competion before playing a game in it! Two seasons after re-entering the competition, Nantwich benefitted from Tranmere Rovers being struck out of it and having defeated Saltney, Middlewich and Whitchurch, a place in the Quarter Finals was landed.

A crowd of 800 was in attendance to see the home clash against Milford Haven United but Nantwich were without star forward Fred Condrey. The Welshman had joined Nantwich from Willaston White Star and went on to play League football with

All Nantwich's results in the Welsh Cup can be accessed on-line. Visit: www.wfda.co.uk/welsh_cup_year_index.php

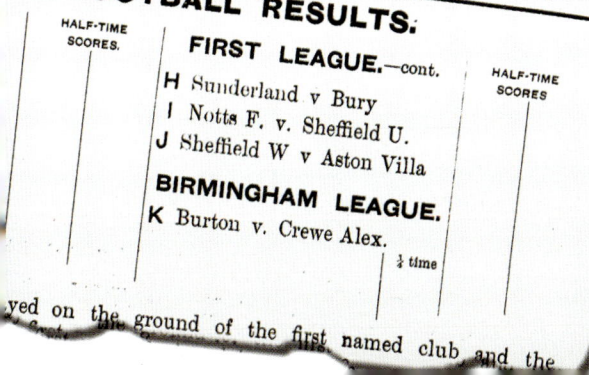

**THE ALEXANDRA NEWS & OFFICIAL PROGRAMME
2 January 1909 (back page)**
Drawn against Crewe Alexandra in the 3rd Round of the Cheshire Senior Cup, Nantwich switched the tie to Gresty Road, hopeful of securing a bigger gate. The experiment paid off with a crowd of 3894, then believed to be a record for the Alex reserves, watching the match. They saw Crewe take the lead and although Jack Forster equalised for Nantwich before the break, the Alex ran out 4-1 winners. So pleased were Nantwich with the gate receipts of £65 18s 11d that when drawn at home to Crewe the following season, the tie was again switched to Gresty Road.

IN THE BEGINNING

Nottingham Forest, but sadly injury ruled him out of the clash. His loss was a big blow and Nantwich's hopes were further dashed in the second half when goalkeeper Ted Steventon's clearance rebounded off the Haven centre-forward and deflected cruelly into the net. Nantwich stepped up a gear and gained four corners in quick succession. The fourth one saw young Albert Ralphs' pinpoint flag kick headed home by skipper Rol White for a crucial equaliser.

Ralphs was a promising Nantwich teenager who also turned out for Burnell's Ironworks and Whitchurch before joining Aston Villa as a 19 year old. He was a right winger and made a single First Division appearance for Villa in the 1911/12 season but moved on to Chester after just a season. He also featured for Mold before a leg injury curtailed his career prematurely. His two younger brothers, Harold and Charlie also played for Nantwich.

For the Welsh Cup replay, Nantwich travelled the 200 miles to South Wales on Friday night but the overnight stay didn't help and they made the long journey back to Cheshire defeated 2-1. It would prove to be Nantwich's last game in the competition as they never again entered the Welsh Cup.

Perhaps the overnight trip to Milford Haven contributed to the club's financial difficulties? Certainly, by the end of the season, the club was £90 in debt and new positions of financial secretaries were created - filled by former Secretary R.E.Walker and T.Boardman. League matches with Crewe Alexandra reserves were still seen as lucrative and so when the Alex shifted their second string from The Combination to the Manchester League in 1910 Nantwich followed suit. After just two seasons a number of Manchester League clubs, Nantwich amongst them, switched to the Lancashire Combination Second Division. The move didn't capture the imagination of the Nantwich sporting public and expenses exceeded gate receipts in all but two league games. Thankfully, a home tie against Crewe in the Cheshire Senior Cup brought in £25 in gate receipts, enabling the books to be balanced by the end of the season.

There was a fair amount of travelling to be done in fulfilling the Lancashire Combination fixtures. Up to Bacup, Lancaster and Barnoldswick and, in the opposite direction, down to Oswestry. There was an amusing incident in April 1914 when Great Harwood came to town. When the referee blew the final whistle, the 3-1 defeat all but ended Harwood's outside chance of winning the league. However, a spectator pointed out to the match official that there was still another seven minutes of the game to play. Standing corrected, the referee re-started the game for a further seven minutes - but without further score on either side.

click4more

All final league tables for the Lancashire Combination Second Division can be viewed on-line. Visit:
www.rsssf.com/tablese/englancacombhist.html#champ2

BACKDROP
The Square, Nantwich soon after the turn of the century.

IN THE BEGINNING

A fortnight later, Nantwich locked horns with Sandbach Ramblers in the Final of the Cheshire Senior Cup. The match was refereed by local footballing hero J.H.Pearson. Pearson had been capped by England in 1892 whilst playing for Crewe Alex and after his playing career ended, he turned to refereeing. He officiated in the 1911 FA Cup Final between Bradford City and Newcastle United and his appointment for the 1914 Cheshire Senior Cup Final was to be his last as a referee. Appropriately enough, the venue was his old stomping ground at Gresty Road.

The Final was a colourful affair with Nantwich wearing claret and the Ramblers in a fetching blue and white kit. Sadly, as the short-lived 'Crewe Observer' pointed out, "the football was not as bright as the colours". Sandbach took an early lead through Reeves and pressed home their advantage when Lambert's speculative effort from near the half-way line ballooned over Ted Steventon in the Nantwich goal. David Beckham would have been proud of it! Just before half-time Simister added a third and the game was as good as over. In the second half, Blackburn, following fine interplay with Chesters, scored with a tremendous drive. It was not enough - Nantwich had fallen to their fourth defeat in as many Senior Cup Finals.

It proved to be one of George Clarke's last games for Nantwich before his transfer to Stoke for a fee of £125 at the age of 20. It wasn't until after the First World War that he figured in Stoke's first team. During the war he had suffered a broken leg whilst serving in France - not from combat but an injury incurred playing army football with the Liverpool Scottish Regiment. A local lad (he was born in Willaston), Clarke was a powerful half-back who made over 150 appearances for Stoke in the early 20s before joining Crewe Alexandra. He remained a part-time footballer throughout his career, and went on to scout for the Alex. He passed away in July 1960.

Missing from the Nantwich line-up in that 1914 Senior Cup Final was George Green. Georgie, who joined the club from Malpas Town, is reputed to be one of the finest forwards ever produced by Nantwich. He later served on the club Committee and, just before and after the Second World War, his son Clarence was a regular in the Nantwich line-up.

Sadly, the dark days of the First World War were now to cast a shadow over the nation and, as elsewhere throughout the land, competitive football in Nantwich went into hibernation. Whether such a devastating war should ever be termed 'Great' is open to question. Millions around the globe lost their lives and, of course, Nantwich - like thousands of places around the planet - had to

1914 CHESHIRE SENIOR CUP FINAL
Runners Up Medal
The Nantwich side that lost 3-1 to Sandbach Ramblers at Crewe on 18th April was: Ted Steventon, F.Poole, Dodd, Billington, George Clarke, Billy Betteley, Stanley Hutton, Blackburn, Chesters, Simms, Jones. Match receipts: £222.

31

IN THE BEGINNING

GEORGE CLARKE
Joined Stoke from Nantwich just before the First World War.

mourn the sad losses of loved ones. Many of those who returned from the trenches were scarred for life - if not physically, then certainly with mental trauma.

Syd Badger was one of those footballers to bear a physical scar. He had enlisted for his country and was wounded in the right knee during the Battle of the River Piave in Italy. Transported back to Britain in a cattle truck, he recovered in Winnington Hospital, Northwich, where the renowned surgeon Major Robert Jones saved his leg. The surgery enabled him to enjoy many seasons playing for Nantwich (and later Oswestry Town). A resident of Ruskin Road in Crewe, he had been an apprentice baker & confectioner with Williams' in Victoria Street before the 'Great War' and, after his recovery, was a baker in Mrs Plumb's shop in Mill Street, Crewe for some 40 years.

Cheshire League days

After the desolation, destruction and despair of the War, belief and hope gradually ushered in a new peacetime era. After such a dreadful war, there was a national yearning for recreation and entertainment. In Nantwich, 'Ye Olde Wyche Theatre' was built in Market Street, overlooking the Church - giving local residents an alternative form of entertainment. In football a new era was also ushered in. Representatives from Nantwich attended a meeting at the Cheshire FA in May 1919 which led to the formation of the Cheshire County League for the forthcoming season.

Nantwich, of course, were one of the original members but, it could be argued, the club was punching above its weight. The fact that the club remained in membership up to the end of the 1937/38 season was a tribute to the industrious Committee members and officials who managed to spend the club's meagre resources with wily care. Time upon time, the local press reported the financial stresses that the club was operating under as Nantwich sought to do battle on a level playing field with the likes of the first teams of, amongst others, Altrincham, Chester, Stalybridge Celtic, Macclesfield, Northwich Victoria and Wigan Athletic. Unsurprisingly, other small clubs fell by the wayside in that inter-war era - Sandbach Ramblers, Middlewich and Whitchurch just some of the names who dropped out of the county league lacking the financial clout to compete.

Yet, like all clubs, Nantwich commenced life in the Cheshire League bathed in optimism. After the dormancy of wartime, the club had re-formed after a public meeting in June 1919. Perhaps the omens should have been heeded at the time - the first meeting had to be cancelled as it was so poorly attended!! At the reconvened meeting, former player Rol White was appointed Secretary and the Chairman (H.Chesworth) moved a vote of thanks to "Mr Gomer Jones for all the good work he had done for the club since 1884", having allowed the club free use of his field off London Road.

An application was made to use the cricket ground at Kingsley Fields, off Welsh Row and the Committee soon busied itself with getting the ground ready for Cheshire League football. The cricket pavilion was to serve as the changing rooms and a wooden stand was erected to provide cover for 500 standing spectators. Ironically, that temporary home was the very site on which the club's new Weaver Stadium was built over 80 years later.

A NEW ERA
Having lain dormant during the First World War, the club sprung back into life at a public meeting held at the Victoria Cocoa House on 25th June 1919. The following elections were made:
Secretary - Roland White,
Chairman & Treasurer - H.Chesworth,
President - Travers Pickmere,
Committee - Messrs Orme, Harris, Tomkinson, Charlie Nicholls, E.Haighton, Garnett, Rollings, G.Egerton, J.Johnson, H.Knowles jnr, J.Williams, E.G.Steventon, A.Hughes, P.Slack, F.Knowles, H.Heaton.

KINGSLEY FIELDS
Local dignatories pictured outside the pavilion at Nantwich Cricket Club's old ground in Kingsley Fields. The pavilion served as changing rooms for the Football Club during its two year residency. The pavilion was replaced by a new one in 1935.

CHESHIRE LEAGUE DAYS

click4more

All final league tables for the Cheshire County League can be viewed on-line. Visit: www.rsssf.com/tablese/engcheshirehist.html#fin1

On 23rd August, the club held its first practice match on the ground to help sift through the 36 players who had been signed on. These included Bayes, Chesters, Green and Knowles (who was appointed captain) who had played for Nantwich before the war. Two goalkeepers had also signed - Harding formerly with Crewe Alex and Frank Birchenough, son of Herbert. The most exciting acquisition was Lal Moses, a tough tackling centre half who had been on Manchester City's books and later went on to manage Winsford United. Billy Weaver was appointed trainer and helped out by playing in the odd game.

A 9-1 pre-season victory over Prees Heath Royal Garrison Artillery was good preparation for the season's opener at Runcorn but despite two goals from Moses, the Wychers slipped to a 4-2 defeat. The first home game was played in the Cheshire League at Kingsley Fields the following week when the return game against Runcorn took place - but the scoreline was the same! Runcorn went on to run away with the Cheshire League title but the rest of the league was a tight affair with Nantwich eventually finishing next to bottom - three points ahead of Northwich Victoria. The highlight was a 5-0 thumping of Chester in the First Qualifying Round of the English Cup; Georgie Green nabbing four of them. Crowd problems which had dogged the club before the war surfaced again and after the 1-1 home draw with Mossley, the Committee appealed for less vile and abusive language to be used on the ground or else they would employ police to expel the offenders.

EDWIN STEVENTON

Born in Bunbury, Ted and his brother Tom played regularly for Nantwich before the Great War and then again in the 20s. Whilst Tom was a centre forward, Ted was a burly goalkeeper who was on the books of Bolton Wanderers and Aston Villa before joining Stoke as an amateur in March 1921. He kept goal three times for the Potters in the League, signing for Wolves as an understudy keeper in May 1922. Throughout this time, he would also play for the Wychers and he also helped out Tettenhall. The Steventon brothers were sons of E.G.Steventon who owned the shoe factory in Barker Street and had been club Treasurer. Both brothers represented the town at cricket and they both served Nantwich Cricket Club as secretary. Ted was a masterly bowler taking over 1000 wickets for Nantwich in the North Staffs & District League in 33 seasons from 1907. Remarkably, in the match against Silverdale in August 1935, he took all 10 wickets. Tom later became headmaster at Bunbury School. In later life, Ted was a Trustee for the Beam Heath land in Nantwich and, like his father, he became a Committee member for Nantwich FC. He was appointed club President after the Second World War and died in March 1971 at the age of 80.

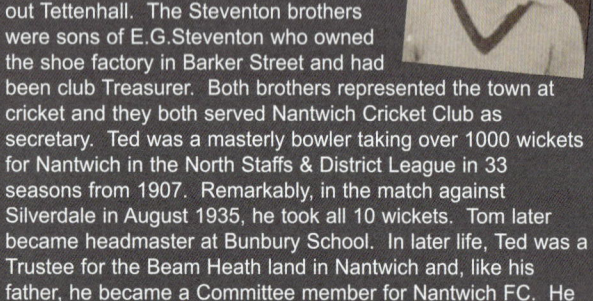

Kingsley Fields was again home the following season and an all-time club record home attendance was set on Saturday 19th February 1921. A week earlier, Nantwich had drawn 2-2 at Winsford United in the Second Round of the Cheshire Senior Cup and, for the replay, an astounding 5121 packed into the ground to see the visitors sneak a 1-0 victory. Interestingly, gate receipts for the match amounted to the grand sum of £193.

The team at the time was full of local players - Ted Steventon, Syd Badger, Jack Slack, 'Niper' Stanley, Ted Edge, Tom Nicholls (whose son Denis played after the Second World War), Georgie Green, Tom Steventon, Herbie Simpson, George Tatton and Frank Mellor.

Jack Slack was something of a character and was reputed to have two pints of beer before playing each match. On a more sinister note, it was alleged that he once sold a match when his back pass flew past Ted Steventon for a spectacular own goal. The allegation was never substantiated.

CHESHIRE LEAGUE DAYS

Left winger Mellor was soon to join Bolton Wanderers for a fee of £230. He made his debut as a 19 year old in the Wanderers' First Division game against Newcastle United in April 1920. He was followed at the end of the following season by Herbie Simpson in a transfer that netted the club a further £300. Simpson made less than a dozen appearances for Bolton, moving on in 1924 to feature more prominently for the old Wigan Borough club (then members of the old Third Division North) and later back to the Cheshire League with Congleton.

So, with hefty transfer fees helping towards a healthy bank balance, the Cobblers returned to the old ground off London Road for the 1921/22 season. The ground had been sown with oats during the war so you can imagine that it took a fair bit of graft to get the playing surface suitable for football again. However, sharing a venue with the cricket club had been causing problems. The overlapping of the football and cricket seasons posed a number of difficulties and the cricket square was getting damaged.

The homecoming to London Road turned out to be something of a damp squib - a goalless Cheshire League draw against Monk's Hall, though gate receipts were a useful £30. It was the only point that Nantwich picked up in their first five games and, come October, the Wychers were next to bottom of the table. A 2-1 home win over Altrincham was followed by a similar win at Macclesfield in front of a crowd of 4000. It sparked a change in fortune and a run of just four defeats in the next 25 games propelled Nantwich up the league. By the end of the campaign, a 6-1 home win over Ashton National cemented a position in sixth place - which proved to be the highest pre-war finish in the Cheshire League.

Gate receipts continued to slide - from £724 in 1921/22 to £655 the following season. Players wages were up, though, from £336 to £545. A Supporters Club was formed for the 1923/24 season with Mr W.T. Galley as its secretary. Although it was a disappointing season in the league, there were decent runs to the Third Qualifying Round of the English Cup and to the semi-finals of the Cheshire Senior Cup. Paired

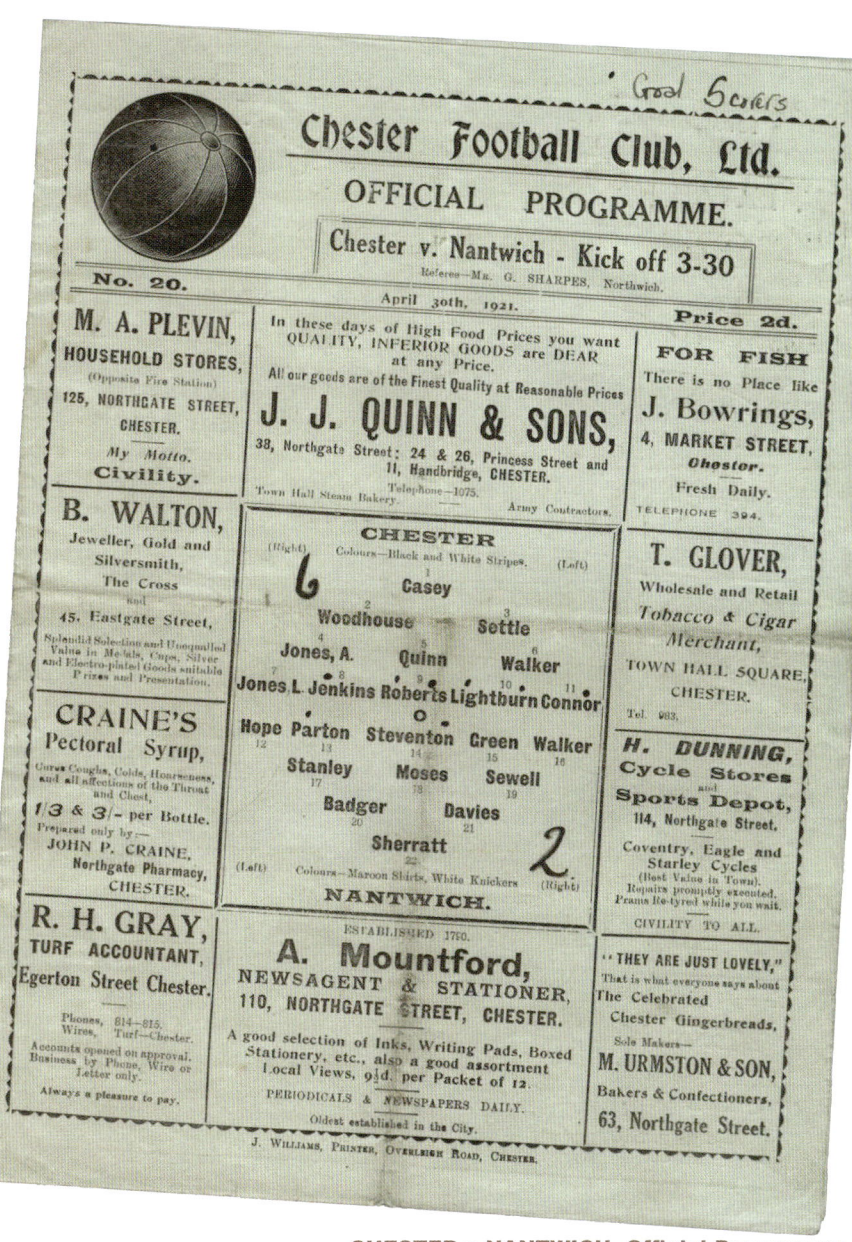

CHESTER v NANTWICH, Official Programme 30 April 1921 (front cover)
Chester's first team competed in the Cheshire League before they were elected to the Football League in 1931. Although Chester won this match 6-2, it was scant revenge for the 9-1 victory that Nantwich had inflicted on them the previous month at Kingsley Fields. Right back Wilf Davies was the son of former Nantwich and Bury footballer Sam, whilst goalscorer Tommy Parton was later transferred to Chester.

NANTWICH FC - 1920/21
Goalkeeper Cecil Sharratt sporting a rather large cap is in the centre of the middle row. Far right (in the top hat) is Secretary Bill Chesworth and, kneeling in front of him, the trainer Tom Clarke. Nantwich finished the season 11th in the Cheshire League.

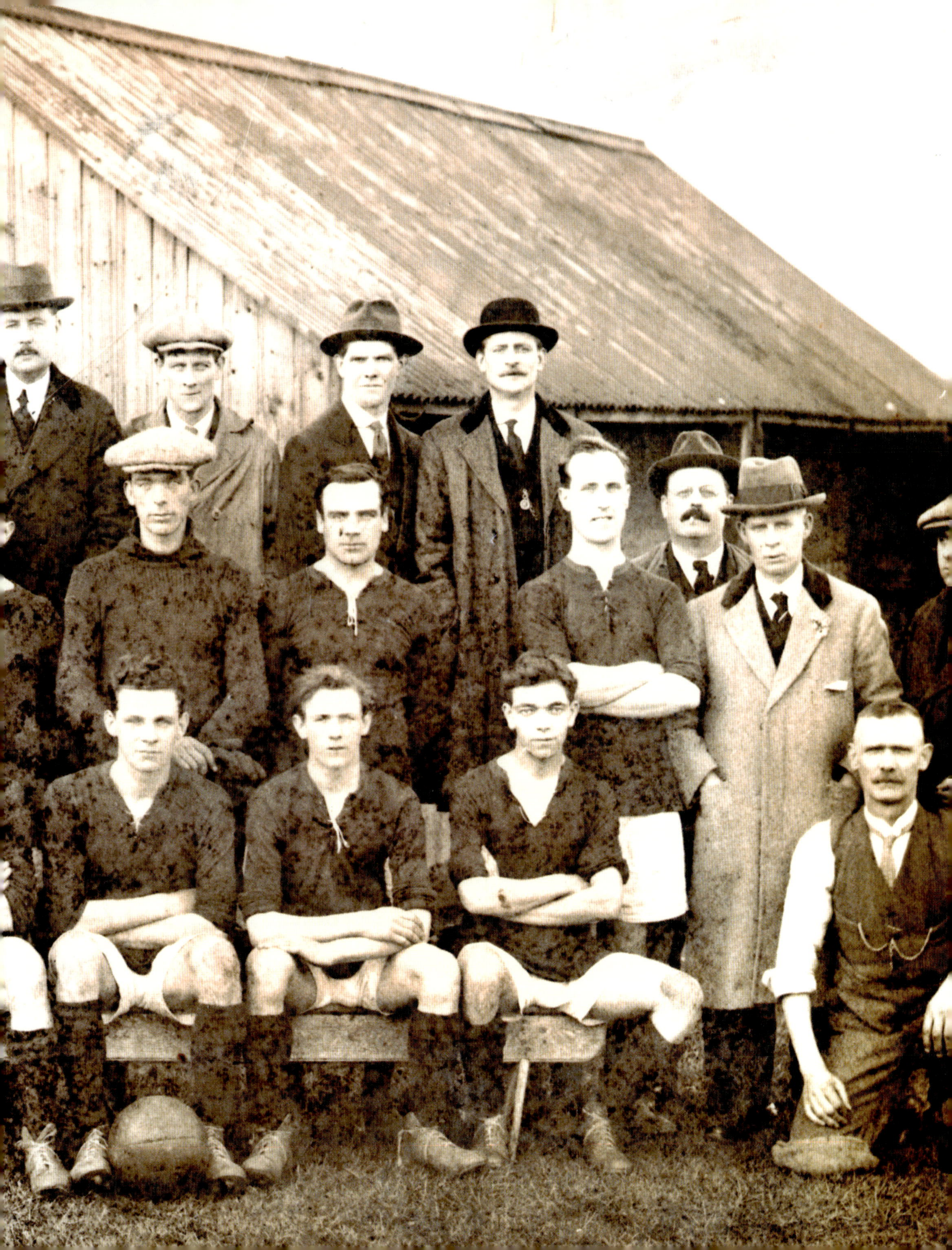

CHESHIRE LEAGUE DAYS

against New Brighton, the Crewe Chronicle reported that a thousand travelling Nantwich fans made the trip to Chester with "all manner of motor vehicles bearing the red & white ribbons of Nantwich." Sadly, they were to return disappointed. Despite a goal from Tom Steventon, Nantwich were beaten 2-1.

Although Nantwich generally struggled to get spectators through the turnstiles, it is amazing to see some of the huge crowds that Cheshire League matches used to pull in back then. Nantwich's match against Crewe Alex Reserves on Good Friday in 1923 had attracted a fantastic crowd of 8243 to Gresty Road. The return matches against the Alex's second string were traditionally held at Nantwich on Easter Monday and the 1924 fixture saw a record 4000 supporters cram into the old London Road ground.

NANTWICH FC - early 1920s
Prolific marksman Georgie Green is in the centre of the front row and the familiar figure of Bill Chesworth is standing second from right.

There was optimism in the camp as the 1924/25 season got under way with former Crewe Alexandra right back Charlie Chorlton taking over the captain's armband. All started well when a Lal Moses penalty and a strike from close season capture Wally Davies, the ex-Crewe Alex forward, earned a 2-1 home win over Stalybridge Celtic on the opening day. Three days later, though, a young lad put the Wychers to the sword. Tranmere Rovers Reserves rolled into town with a dynamic forward earning rave reviews amongst local commentators. Billy Dean had signed from local Wirral side Pensby Institute and had already netted in Rovers' 5-2 win over Nantwich at Prenton Park the previous season. On his visit to Nantwich, the 17 year old shone like a beacon and Rovers returned to the Wirral with a 4-2 victory - all four goals coming from the boot of the fabled Dixie Dean who went on to become an Everton legend. The Nantwich faithful that afternoon were getting an early glimpse of a football genius who remains, to this day, one of the best ever strikers in the history of the game. Dean secured 16 England caps in an era where international matches were few and far between and his record-breaking haul of 60 League goals for the Toffees in 1927/28 is unlikely ever to be beaten.

DIXIE DEAN
The Everton legend who tormented Nantwich as a youngster with Tranmere reserves.

Despite attendances generally being poor, there was much local interest in the team's performances. When Nantwich played away from home, a telegram carrying the match result would be sent to Gilbert's (a tobacconist's on the corner of Oat Market and

CHESHIRE LEAGUE DAYS

Swine Market) where it was displayed enabling assembled supporters to find out how their team had fared. Granted, not quite the Sky Sports Videprinter!

Competing against some of the best non-league sides in the North was starting to take its financial toll on the club and in March 1925, it was reported that £200 to £250 was needed just for the club to complete the season. "The meagre attendances week-by-week at the London-road enclosure have greatly discouraged the committee," reported the Chronicle. "A satisfactory team cannot be secured with such scant support," it added before finishing off bluntly: "Plainly stated the club's existence is at stake."

HARRY BOSTON

An old fashioned forward with bags of League experience, Harry scored Nantwich's only goal in the 1933 Cheshire Senior Cup Final - arguably one of the most important strikes in the club's history. Born in Nantwich in October 1899, Harry (or Henry James to be precise) worked for Haighton's before the First World War intervened and he joined up with the South Lancashire Regiment. Continuing in the army after cessation of hostilities, Harry was asked to turn out for Nantwich reserves against Alpraham & Calveley on Christmas Day morning in 1921 whilst on Christmas leave. He did, at centre-forward, and scored 8 times!

"They wanted me to play for the Cheshire League side in the afternoon," Harry later recalled. "But I had a sore throat and had to refuse. That was my only appearance in the Reserves and when I finally left the Army the following March, I played regularly in the first team."

It wasn't long before Harry attracted the attention of Bolton Wanderers. Manager Charles Foweraker took him to Burnden Park in 1923 where Harry earned the princely sum of £8 a week in the winter - £6 a week in the summer - with a £2 bonus for a win and a £1 bonus for a draw! Six weeks after joining, he was thrown into the fray, making his First Division debut against Aston Villa. An ankle injury deprived him of a place in Wanderers' 1929 FA Cup winning line-up after his work on the wing had helped the Trotters progress through earlier rounds.

Then, in 1930/31, West Bromwich Albion boss Fred Everiss lured Harry to the Hawthorns for a £2000 fee - quite a sum in those days. He helped Albion to promotion to the First Division at the end of his second season but then moved on to Swansea Town. He had just one season in South Wales. "I decided I'd had enough," he said in later life, returning to his native Nantwich and re-joining the town club.

He had suffered a torn knee ligament but despite the risk of further injury, he happily turned out for the Dabbers. Before each match, eleven yards of bandage was strapped around his leg. "It used to take me two hours to get them off afterwards," he joked, "usually with the skin as well!"

Playing through the pain barrier in the 1933 Cheshire Senior Cup Final paid off for Nantwich, though, and Boston's lightning drive past ICI Alkali 'keeper Lees was a defining moment in Nantwich's long football history. He finally decided to call it a day at the end of that season but continued to take an interest in football - and boxing. He kept a close eye on the boxing career of his nephew Jackie Potts, who became licensee of The Leopard in Nantwich. A renowned sprinter in his youth, Harry became a storekeeper-driver for G.F. & A. Brown Ltd, the wine and spirit merchants, after he hung up his football boots. He died in 1973.

NANTWICH RESERVES
Crewe & District League Champions 1922/23
Back Row (left to right): Tom Clarke (trainer), Alf Jones (Secretary), Stan Dean, Arnold Adams, Trickett, Charlie Nicholls.
Middle Row: Fred Heath, Hector McBride, Charlie Chesworth.
Front Row: Harold Ralphs (sporting his Cheshire FA badge), Arthur Mullock, Bill Mason, Walter Butler, Cecil Sharratt.

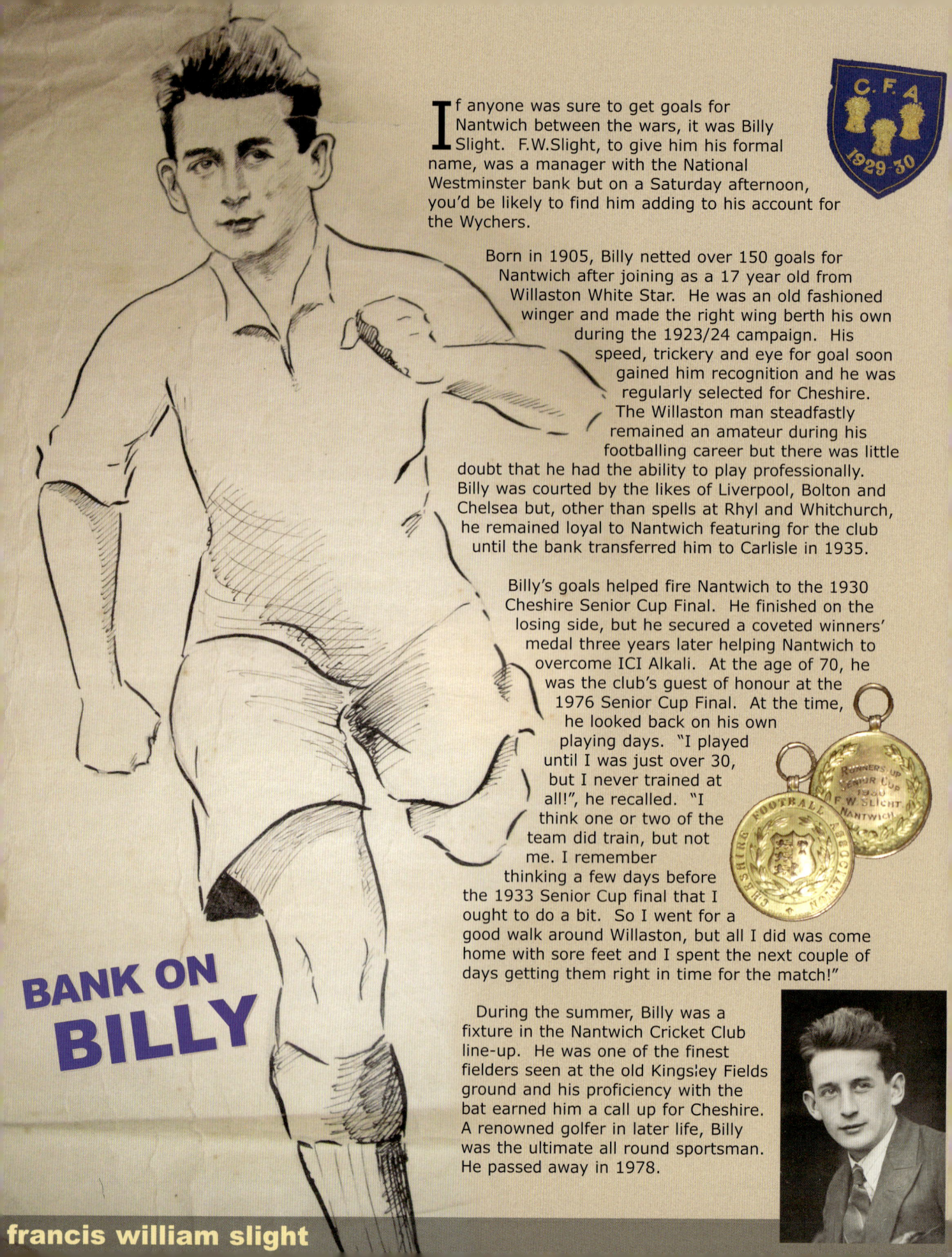

If anyone was sure to get goals for Nantwich between the wars, it was Billy Slight. F.W.Slight, to give him his formal name, was a manager with the National Westminster bank but on a Saturday afternoon, you'd be likely to find him adding to his account for the Wychers.

Born in 1905, Billy netted over 150 goals for Nantwich after joining as a 17 year old from Willaston White Star. He was an old fashioned winger and made the right wing berth his own during the 1923/24 campaign. His speed, trickery and eye for goal soon gained him recognition and he was regularly selected for Cheshire. The Willaston man steadfastly remained an amateur during his footballing career but there was little doubt that he had the ability to play professionally. Billy was courted by the likes of Liverpool, Bolton and Chelsea but, other than spells at Rhyl and Whitchurch, he remained loyal to Nantwich featuring for the club until the bank transferred him to Carlisle in 1935.

Billy's goals helped fire Nantwich to the 1930 Cheshire Senior Cup Final. He finished on the losing side, but he secured a coveted winners' medal three years later helping Nantwich to overcome ICI Alkali. At the age of 70, he was the club's guest of honour at the 1976 Senior Cup Final. At the time, he looked back on his own playing days. "I played until I was just over 30, but I never trained at all!", he recalled. "I think one or two of the team did train, but not me. I remember thinking a few days before the 1933 Senior Cup final that I ought to do a bit. So I went for a good walk around Willaston, but all I did was come home with sore feet and I spent the next couple of days getting them right in time for the match!"

During the summer, Billy was a fixture in the Nantwich Cricket Club line-up. He was one of the finest fielders seen at the old Kingsley Fields ground and his proficiency with the bat earned him a call up for Cheshire. A renowned golfer in later life, Billy was the ultimate all round sportsman. He passed away in 1978.

BANK ON BILLY

francis william slight

CHESHIRE LEAGUE DAYS

A meeting at the Victoria Temperance Hotel took the brave decision that the club should carry on. The ground at the time was not owned by the club so, without any assets to speak of, Wesley Emberton (Chairman of the rugby club) and Henry Knowles offered to become guarantors. Secretary Billy Williamson pointed out that gate receipts averaged only about £20 a match. The club clearly couldn't afford the ten paid players on its books so it was sensibly agreed to continue in the Cheshire League but as basically an amateur side.

Two months later, the old Committee stood down and although there was talk of the club being formed into a Limited Company, a new committee was elected with Rupert Harvey as President, Harry Bowker as Secretary and H.Owen as Treasurer.

With things looking up, six 'professionals' were engaged for the start of the 1925/26 campaign - goalkeeper Frank Birchenough, Charlie Chorlton, Albert Sewell (who went on to serve Crewe Alex), Tommy Parton (the former Chester striker), ex-Whitchurch midfielder H.R.Dawson and winger George Tatton. Tatton's name, according to the local paper, "is almost synonymous with Nantwich football." It went on to note that his "long legs and terrific drives were bound to bring him into the limelight." They weren't wrong. 'The Flyer', as Nantwich fans dubbed him, had a trial with Huddersfield Town in May 1923 and later had a spell with Bolton Wanderers but was unable to force a place in the first team. 'Tat', whose first name was actually Alfred, was a favourite with the Nantwich fans who could be heard yelling 'Give it to Tat'. He resided in Walthall Street, Crewe and had sadly lost his brother in the Great War.

NANTWICH FC - 1925/26
Pictured in front of the old changing rooms at the London Road ground. Billy Slight is seated second from right, trainer Tom Clarke standing far right.

By now Billy Slight had become a regular on the scoresheet. Slight was something of a fixture in the Nantwich line-up until the outbreak of World War Two, unsurprisingly being appointed club captain. It was acknowledged that he could have gone on to play at a higher level. However, he had a good job as a local Bank Manager so the unpredictability of professional football never tempted him. Jim Kettle, Nantwich's stalwart fan who started following his home town team back in the 30s, remembers Slight as one of the best players ever to play for Nantwich.

That 1925/26 season saw the Wychers finish a creditable 8th in the Cheshire League but the following years saw the club gradually slip down the table and, as it did so, the club's financial position deteriorated again.

This wasn't helped by the old grandstand being blown over twice in two years. It had been partially weakened by a storm in January 1927 which had cost the club £22 in repairs. Then, a year later

CHESHIRE LEAGUE DAYS

A CANTERBURY LAMB
Offered to the club in 1928 as a means to help raise funds.

WYCHERS, COBBLERS & DABBERS

In its early years, Nantwich FC's nickname was 'The Saltmen' or 'The Wychers' in recognition of the town's heritage in the salt industry. The town also had a vibrant shoe-making industry so the team was also referred to as 'The Cobblers'. It was not until the 1930s that the unusual nickname 'The Dabbers' came into vogue. Anyone from Nantwich is known as a 'Dabber' but strangely nobody knows the precise origin of the nickname. It is believed to come from the tanning industry which had a strong presence in Nantwich. In the tanneries, leather hides were dabbed with salt or acid as part of the tanning process and the person who did this was called a 'Dabber'.

Another explanation - perhaps less plausible - is that the workers who built the half-timbered houses prevalent around the town were called 'daubers' because of the 'wattle and daub' wall frame fillings. It is suggested that at some point 'dauber' could have become 'Dabber'.

After the Second World War the club was also known as 'The Lilywhites', inspired by the white jerseys worn at the time, but it has continued to be affectionately referred to by that unique nickname - 'The Dabbers'.

another £19 had to be forked out after it had been damaged by further strong winds. To make matters worse, the dressing rooms were dilapidated and, at the league's insistence, these were brought up to scratch - costing another £14. A further £25 was spent carrying out repairs to the fence round the ground so that by early 1928, the club's debts had shot up to £183.

Club Chairman, H.Massey had resigned because of the situation and the new Chairman, Thomas Wood, warned that the outlook wasn't good. "I don't want the club to go down but it looks like extinction unless assistance from the public is forthcoming." A Public Appeal was launched to raise funds and Whist Drives and rummage sales planned to raise cash. Crewe Alexandra donated £10 and an appeal went out for 30 people to each donate £5 and for a further 50 people to raise 20 shillings each. The local press reported that a Mr Schofield offered the club a Canterbury lamb to be used in raising funds!

The appeal was a success. The club raised £174 and a list of subscribers was gratefully posted in the window of Gilberts, the tobacconist's.

Thankfully, the club pulled through but a tightening of the belt meant that there was little money to attract players - and the club's better players were quick to move on. One youngster starting to make an impression was Freddie Worrall. He was signed by Oldham Athletic in December 1928, heralding a career that would see him feature in two FA Cup finals for Portsmouth - and gain two caps for his country. To this day, Worrall remains the only Nantwich player who has gone on to play for England at full international level.

Despite young Worrall's presence, Nantwich lost the opening seven Cheshire League games of the 1928/29 season, including a 9-1 reverse at Ashton National in front of a crowd of 6000 and 7-2 home defeats at the hands of Port Vale Reserves and Sandbach Ramblers. Although there was some improvement in results mid-season, the Dabbers lost their last thirteen league games and ended up propping up the table - conceding a mammoth 159 goals in the process.

Fortunately, there was to be some relief the following season in the Cheshire Senior Cup. By defeating Neston Brickworks (7-1 at home), Middlewich and Sandbach Ramblers (both after replays), the Dabbers came face to face with Tranmere Rovers in the Semi-Finals at Crewe. Rain and snow had turned the Gresty Road pitch into a quagmire but Nantwich were put at a disadvantage when heavy smoke was emitted from the adjoining railway. With vision partially obscured, Rovers made the most of the smokescreen with Watts scoring past a bewildered Nantwich defence! Frank Davies, signed from Portsmouth at the start of the season, equalised with a fine shot. Then, in the second half, Billy Slight was brought down and Jack Harris converted the spot kick to put the Dabbers through to the Final.

ENGLAND INTERNATIONAL

Freddie Worrall may not be a name that slips off the tongues of today's young footy fans but before the war, he was one of the country's top players. Freddie had briefly been on the books of Witton Albion but it was at Nantwich that he was groomed for a career that would see him play at the top level - and twice play for England.

Freddie Worrall had joined the Wychers in the 1925/26 season. He was soon given his first team chance but, perhaps unsurprisingly, he struggled to make an impact. When Nantwich lost 2-1 at Ellesmere Port in April 1926, the local paper had reported that Worrall "was thrustful, but his shots were not dangerous." Mind you, the lad was only 15!! Who'd have thought he'd go on to become an England international?!

The young forward matured quickly. By the following season, the same paper was praising him: "Worrall displayed great capabilities as the leader of the attack". Young Freddie lived in Warrington, and was brought to games on the back of teammate Jack Harris' motorbike.

Despite playing in a side struggling in the Cheshire League, Worrall's potential clearly shone through as he developed into a tricky right winger. It wasn't long before the big boys came knocking. Just turned 18, he signed for First Division giants Bolton Wanderers on 5th November 1928. That was just when the fireworks started, though!

The FA deemed the transfer was illegal. Worrall had been turning out for Nantwich as an amateur. He signed professional forms for Nantwich on the day of his transfer to Bolton so that the club could receive a fee for him (Bolton paid the princely sum of £250). But the FA threw the rulebook at Bolton – saying Wanderers had paid a transfer fee for an amateur and that, apparently, was bang out of order.

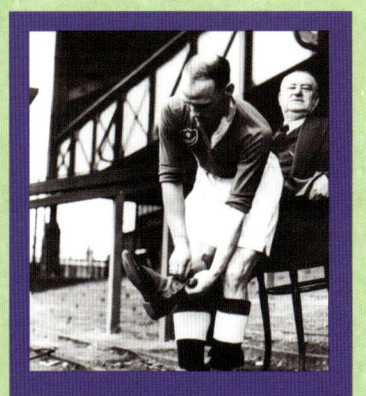

The transfer was cancelled and Nantwich had to pay back the £250. Bolton were fined £50 and barred from signing the player. Although the FA made no criticism of Nantwich, it didn't stop them slapping a £20 fine on the club – a hefty sum in those days.

But, as the saying goes, you can't keep a good man down. A month later, Worrall was snapped up by Second Divison Oldham. He made over 100 appearances for the Latics before moving to First Division high-fliers Portsmouth. He played in two FA Cup Finals (1934 & 1939), setting up two goals for Cliff Parker in their surprise 1939 success. Whilst with Pompey, he was selected for his country, gaining a couple of England caps in the mid-30s, and also twice playing for the Football League in representative matches.

Freddie was one of those footballers who clung to a string of superstitions. He never travelled without his lucky charms and took all five of them on the field at Wembley when he turned out for Pompey in the 1939 Cup Final. He carried a small horseshoe in his pocket, pushed a sprig of white heather down each sock, tied a small white elephant to one of his garters and put a lucky sixpence in his boot!

After the war, Freddie played for Crewe Alexandra and then joined Stockport County. After retiring from playing, he coached Chester, trained Warrington Rugby League club and managed Stockton Heath FC for 12 years after they joined the Mid-Cheshire League.

SPATMAN Worrall's Portsmouth had surprised everyone by reaching the 1939 FA Cup Final. In an early round, Manager Jack Tinn had walked into the dressing room wearing a pair of spats – fabric shoe covers that were popular at the time. Pompey won the game. After that, the spats were kept in a safe between rounds and, before each game, superstitious Freddie would ceremoniously tie the spats onto Tinn's shoes! The superstitions paid off – Portsmouth hammered hot favourites Wolves 4-1 in the Final.

Frederick J Worrall

Born Warrington, 8 September 1910. Died 1979

League Career
Oldham Athletic 1928-31 105 appearances (21 goals)
Portsmouth 1931-38 316 apps (69 goals)
Crewe Alexandra 1946/7 6 apps (1 goal)

England Caps
Holland 0 England 1 (Amsterdam, 18 May 1935)
England 3 Northern Ireland 1 (Stoke, 18 November 1936)
Worrall scored in both games.

CHESHIRE LEAGUE DAYS

The day of the 1930 Cheshire Senior Cup Final saw all roads to Crewe blocked as virtually the whole town of Nantwich made the short trip to watch a repeat of the Senior Cup Final 40 years earlier. As they had been in 1890, Nantwich were underdogs to a strong Macclesfield side riding high in the Cheshire League. Never before (or since) had there been so much excitement about a Nantwich match. Gresty Road was full to the rafters - literally! Fans gained whatever vantage point they could - including perching on top of the stand roof. By kick off, there was nearly 15,000 in the ground. Nantwich fans had gathered behind the railway end goal, sporting berets and tam-o-shanters in the club colours of red and black. The Macclesfield fans were decked out in blue and white with umbrellas, top hats, coloured caps and rattles, with musical instruments all adding to the fervour of the occasion. The Macclesfield Jazz band added a touch of razmatazz to the proceedings and a raucous cheer went up from the Nantwich faithful when their heroes took to the field - most of them local lads.

Thompson, the goalkeeper, had been with Bolton Wanderers as an amateur and was selected to play for the Cheshire League against the Welsh League that season. He later joined Manchester United but failed to make the grade at Old Trafford. There was another Thompson (unrelated) at right back, a policeman from Bunbury. Left back Joe Astley had joined the club a few months earlier and had tasted League football with Manchester United and Notts County. Right half Ernie Davies later became the landlord of The Badger pub

1930 CHESHIRE SENIOR CUP FINAL
12 April 1930 at Crewe
Nantwich 4, Macclesfield 5

Pictured below, Billy Johnston (right) running forward after his shot passed through Albert Sewell's legs into the net to give Macclesfield the lead. Macc's Stanton and Taylor are seen on the left.
Nantwich: T.Thompson, C.Thompson, Joseph Astley, Ernie Davies, Andy Blake, Albert Sewell, Leonard Mason, Frank Davies, Jack Harris, Billy Slight, Harold Robinson.
Scorers: Harris 2, F.Davies 2
Attendance: 14,647
Receipts: £802 13s

44

at Church Minshull and his half-back partners, Andy Blake and Albert Sewell, were both ex-Crewe Alexandra men. Sewell was actually in his second spell with Nantwich, having originally left the Dabbers for the Alex in 1927. He gave up his football career in the 1930s due to a re-occurence of a leg injury and sadly lost his sight in later life. Blake, a no-nonsense Scotsman from West Lothian, would become the club's trainer just after the Second World War. Jack Harris had played for Runcorn and, as well as leading the line, could fill in at centre half. Outside left Harold Robinson was proprietor of a shoe shop in Beam Street whilst the players were trained and managed by 'Dip' Hassall. Dip was a long standing servant to the club, going on to clock up over 45 years service. He had started out as goalkeeper back in 1887 and represented Cheshire before joining Bacup in 1894. Ironically, he had been in goal in that 1890 Final against Macc - who he was later to play for. Dip was something of a character. Just before the team went on the field, he always shouted in his broad accent, "Are ye alreet?". He was a strong believer of whisky as a remedy for knocks and had the charming habit of taking a swig of whisky, swilling it around in his mouth and spitting it out onto the injured player's leg! The medical jury is out on whether or not it helped the player - but it sure made Dip feel better!

Dip would have been disappointed with the start Nantwich made to the 1930 Final. Having had the better of early skirmishes, they let in Macclesfield captain Billy Johnston to put the Silkmen one up on the quarter hour. But Dip's troops hit back and Harris headed home an equaliser from Robinson's pinpoint cross. Better was to come when Davies' splendid shot gave the Cobblers an unexpected half-time lead. After the break, the Silkmen rallied. Johnston added a second and then completed his hat-trick. Former Oldham winger Cliff Stanton put Macc 4-2 up before Johnston added his fourth - and Macc's fifth. But Nantwich kept going and Harris reduced the arrears with six minutes left on the clock. Then Davies notched his second with a spectacular overhead kick, leaving Macc hanging on for dear life and, in great desperation, they held out the last couple of minutes to record a thrilling 5-4 victory.

The heart breaking defeat - Nantwich's fifth in as many Senior Cup finals - set the tone for a disappointing campaign the following season with the Cobblers finishing next to bottom of the Cheshire League. The 1931/32 season was worse still - wooden spoonists and conceding 155 goals! There was just one league win all season - a surprisingly comfortable 6-3 beating of Hurst at the beginning of January. There was a welcome boost to finances, though, when

**CHESTER v NANTWICH
24 January 1931**
How the Chronicle cartoonist saw Chester's comfortable 5-1 win over Nantwich. The Cestrians finished runners-up in the Cheshire League at the end of the season and were elected to the Football League.

HEAVIEST DEFEATS

2-16 v Stalybridge Celtic (away) 1932/33 Cheshire County League, 22 Oct 1932
0-13 v Tranmere Rovers Reserves (away) 1937/38 Cheshire County League, 7 Apr 1938
0-12 v Runcorn (away) 1936/37 Cheshire County League, 26 Sept 1936
0-12 v Northwich Victoria (away) 1893/94 Cheshire Senior Cup 1st Rd, 11 Nov 1893
0-12 v Chirk (away) 1888/89 English Cup 2nd Rd Qual, 27 Oct 1888
0-11 v Hyde United (away) 1933/34 Cheshire County League, 16 Sept 1933
1-11 v Barnton (away) 1954/55 Mid-Cheshire League
3-11 v Congleton Town (home) 1936/37 Cheshire County League, 23 Sept 1936
0-10 v Northwich Victoria (away) 1994/95 FA Cup 2nd Rd Qual, 24 Sept 1994
0-10 v Stoke Swifts (away) 1893/94 The Combination, 23 Dec 1893
0-10 v Everton Reserve (away) 1892/93 The Combination, 17 Sept 1892
1-10 v Droylsden United (away) 1949/50 FA Cup Prel Rd, 17 Sept 1949
1-10 v Stockport County Reserves (away) 1927/28 Cheshire County League, 14 Jan 1928
2-10 v Stockton Heath (away) Mid-Cheshire League 1956/57
2-10 v ICI (Alkali) (away) 1938/39 Crewe & District Amateur League, 24 Sept 1938
3-10 v Stalybridge Celtic (away) 1933/34 Cheshire County League, 17 Apr 1934
0-9 v Crewe Alexandra (away) 2000/01 Cheshire Senior Cup Prel Rd, 30 Sept 2000
0-9 v Ellesmere Port Town (away) 1946/47 FA Cup Prel Rd, 21 Sept 1946
0-9 v Everton Reserve (home) 1892/93 The Combination, 3 Sept 1892
1-9 v Witton Albion (away) 1978/79 Cheshire League Div 1, 9 Dec 1978
1-9 v Knutsford (away) 1958/59 Mid-Cheshire League
1-9 v Ashton Naional (away) 1928/29 Cheshire County League, 8 Sept 1928
1-9 v Tranmere Rovers (away) 1909/10 The Combination, 18 Dec 1909
1-9 v Oswestry United (away) 1906/07 The Combination, 24 Nov 1906
1-9 v Wharton Parish (away) 1894/95 Cheshire Junior League, 6 April 1895
2-9 v Rhyl (away) 1935/36 FA Cup Prel Rd, 21 Sept 1935
2-9 v Ashton National (away) 1931/32 Cheshire County League, 29 Aug 1931
3-9 v Sandbach Ramblers (away) 1958/59 Cheshire Senior Cup 2nd Qual Rd
3-9 v Hurst (away) 1932/33 Cheshire County League, 25 Apr 1933
3-9 v Hurst (away) 1928/29 Cheshire County League, 24 Nov 1928
3-9 v Burscough (away) 1993/94 NW Counties League Div 1, 7 Apr 1994

Bower Fold
Home of Stalybridge Celtic - pictured between the wars

Stalybridge ended their short two year stint in the Football League in 1923 when their first team replaced their reserves in the Cheshire League. From then on, Nantwich suffered a catastrophic series of results on their visits to Bower Fold:
23/24 0-6 24/25 0-7 25/26 2-3 26/27 1-4 27/28 2-4 28/29 1-5
29/30 1-2 30/31 3-4 31/32 2-4 32/33 2-16 33/34 3-10 34/35 1-6
35/36 1-8 36/37 0-8 37/38 0-7

Given a home tie against Stalybridge in January 1932 in the Cheshire Senior Cup, Nantwich switched the Second Round tie to Bower Fold in return for being guaranteed gate receipts of £35. Celtic, of course, could virtually guarantee the result - they won 8-4!
During this period, Nantwich's horrendous record at Bower Fold was:
P16 W0 D0 L16 F23 A101.

CHESHIRE LEAGUE DAYS

Manchester City paid £700 to sign promising left winger Blair in November 1931. The 22 year old, an athletics master at a Liverpool school, had also been watched by Arsenal but unfortunately did not make the break through at Maine Road.

There was scant improvement the following season and on 22nd October 1932, the Nantwich team returned from Stalybridge Celtic on the back of a 16-2 hiding - it remains the club's heaviest defeat in any competition. Albert Pinxton and Len Butt got Nantwich's goals; Stalybridge's scorers - too numerous to mention!

Despite disappointing results in the league, Nantwich put together a decent run in the Cheshire Senior Cup again. The Cheshire FA had banned Football League clubs from entering the Senior Cup as the clubs had been supplementing their reserve sides with first team ringers. Without the likes of Crewe Alexandra, Tranmere Rovers and Chester in the competition, Cheshire League clubs fancied their chances of glory.

The Wychers needed a replay to overcome Winsford United in the First Round and in the Second Round a brace from Billy Slight was instrumental in defeating Sandbach Ramblers 4-0. This set up an intriguing semi-final against Northern Nomads at Crewe's Gresty Road ground. When Nomads failed to clear Len Butt's corner, Cyrus Johnson pounced to give Nantwich the lead but ten minutes before the break, Griffiths equalised. Just after the hour mark, Frank Simon restored Nantwich's lead from the penalty spot but Griffiths again levelled for Nomads. Then, in the last minute, Johnson got the final touch on a scramble in front of the Nomads' goal to give Nantwich a pulsating 3-2 win.

The opponents in the Final were to be ICI Alkali - a club that had been formed from the ashes of the old Winnington Park side that Nantwich had beaten in the 1896 Cheshire Junior Cup Final. Members of the Manchester League, all ICI's players were amateurs and employees of the company. They had won through, against the odds, by defeating Cheshire League sides Hyde United and Macclesfield on the way to the Final. Coached by former Manchester City and Norwich City centre-half Sydney Scott, they were a young side with an average age of just 21. They would be no easy touch.

NORTHERN NOMADS v NANTWICH
Cheshire Senior Cup Semi-Final at Crewe
Centre page line-ups from the official programme

MANCHESTER CENTRAL 7 NANTWICH 0
27 February 1932
Programme from the only time Nantwich played Manchester Central's first team at Belle Vue. Central had a short history, being founded in 1928 by former Manchester City Director John Ayrton who was disappointed that City had located its new ground at Maine Road and not in its east Manchester heartlands. Set up with the express aim of joining the Football League, Manchester football hero Billy Meredith was appointed as Manager. After their third application to join the Football League was defeated in 1931, Central withdrew their first team from the Lancashire Combination to take up their reserves' place in the Cheshire League. Central finished the campaign in 5th place but, with their dreams of the Football League unrealised, they folded at the end of the season.

STALYBRIDGE CELTIC 16 NANTWICH 2
Cheshire League
22 October 1932
The Chronicle match report sums up the club's record defeat in a few column inches ... say no more!

47

CHESHIRE LEAGUE DAYS

CHESHIRE SENIOR CUP FINAL
Drill Field, Northwich

Nantwich fans celebrate the club winning the Cheshire Senior Cup for the first time. Along the front row (from right to left) are Walter Weaver, Tommy Ormes, Harold Davis and, next but one, Billy Lawton. The tall man in the hat peeping over Tommy's head is Bill Taylor and the little boy on the left with the clenched fist is Bunny Hodgkiss. Sixth from left is Albert Nicholls who went on to play for the Dabbers. After the war, Albert played alongside his nephew, Denis Nicholls, whilst his brother Tom took over as the club's trainer in 1947.

And so it proved. On a warm, sunny April afternoon, a crowd of 8000 assembled at the Drill Field, home of Northwich Victoria, and they cheered the sides as they both entered the arena. Nantwich were decked out in their black and amber stripes whilst ICI's dark blue and pale blue quarters were more akin to racing colours. Nantwich were without Albert Pinxton who had broken his arm but otherwise were at full strength. Pinxton's absence was a big loss. He was a promising inside right who joined Blackburn Rovers a month later. Young John (later Doctor) Turner who had just returned from studying medicine at Cambridge University also missed the match.

The game was a lively affair with neither side managing to stamp their impression on the game. Cyrus Johnson rattled the bar with an early free kick and Nantwich nearly took the lead when Hayes almost turned the ball into his own net. The 'Chemics' then pressed and Herrod was called upon to tip a sizzler from Williams over the bar. Eight minutes into the second half, the deadlock was finally broken. Frank Simon slotted the ball into the path of Harry Boston who fired past Chemics' keeper Lees from outside the penalty area.

Len Butt had a chance to double the lead but, as the clock ticked down, it was Nantwich who were left to desperately hold on. Allen shot inches wide, Thompson almost got the better of Herrod on a one-on-one and, with tension mounting, Hughes scooped the ball high over the bar when he should have levelled matters from close range. At last the final whistle went. Nantwich had won 1-0 and, after years of trying, they at last lifted the Cheshire Senior Cup.

A huge cheer went up as the trophy was presented by Ted Case, Chairman of the Cheshire FA, to Nantwich skipper Frank 'Doffey' Simon. Hughes, the ICI captain, sportingly called for three cheers for Nantwich and the victory signalled widespread celebration in the town.

When the team arrived back, there was a great reception awaiting them on the Barony. The cup was taken to the club's headquarters, the Liberal Club, and afterwards was proudly on show at the captain's house.

Such was the excitement that one man hobbled into The Leopard on crutches to celebrate but happily walked home unaided at closing time. It was more a case that the man had been swinging the lead rather than Senior Cup euphoria proffering a miracle cure!

Some shops were closed for up to a week as the town marked the success of its football team which, of course, was mainly made up of local players. The longest serving was Billy Slight - the only survivor from the team that lost the 1930 Final. A few did have Football League experience. Right back Vic Fox had been with Middlesbrough and Wolves and had also played county cricket for Worcestershire. He was Nantwich Cricket Club's professional for a number of seasons. Cyrus Johnson would go on to taste League football with New Brighton and had returned to the country after a spell serving in the Canadian Mounted Police. Harry Boston had started out with Nantwich and returned to the club after serving Bolton Wanderers, West Bromwich Albion and Swansea Town. Right half Ernie Platt was a Willaston lad and, like Slight, played for the county as an amateur. He had lost two fingers, trapping them in a machine in an accident at Crewe Works. Mountford, who had been signed from Sneyd Colliery FC, tragically collapsed and

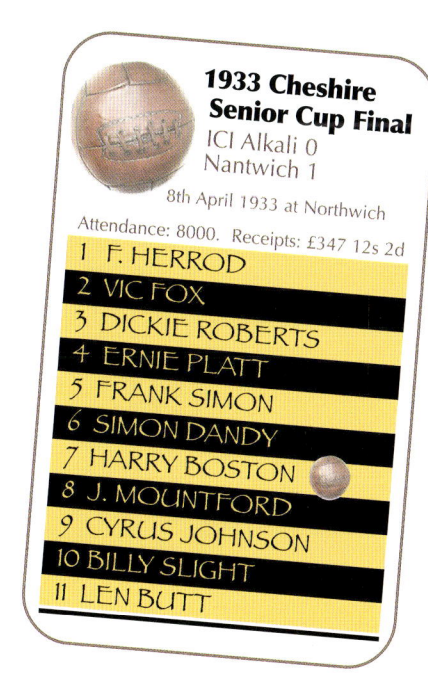

1933 Cheshire Senior Cup Final
ICI Alkali 0
Nantwich 1
8th April 1933 at Northwich
Attendance: 8000. Receipts: £347 12s 2d

1 F. HERROD
2 VIC FOX
3 DICKIE ROBERTS
4 ERNIE PLATT
5 FRANK SIMON
6 SIMON DANDY
7 HARRY BOSTON
8 J. MOUNTFORD
9 CYRUS JOHNSON
10 BILLY SLIGHT
11 LEN BUTT

NANTWICH FC - Cheshire Senior Cup Winners 1933
Players and Committee members pictured before the game against Whitchurch - the club's first after winning the 1933 Cheshire Senior Cup Final
Standing (left to right): Albert Pinxton, Colin Chesters (Vice-Chairman), Ernie Platt, Mr Rogers, Vic Fox, Mr Stanley Davies, F.Herrod, Mr G.Hancock, Frank Simon, Mr A.Knowles, Simon Dandy, Mr Frank Farrington, John Turner, Mr W.R.Parham, Dickie Roberts
Front Row: Harry Bowker (Secretary), Harry Boston, J.Mountford, Cyrus Johnson, Billy Slight, Len Butt, Walter Cooper (Trainer). Mascot: Kenny Carrol.

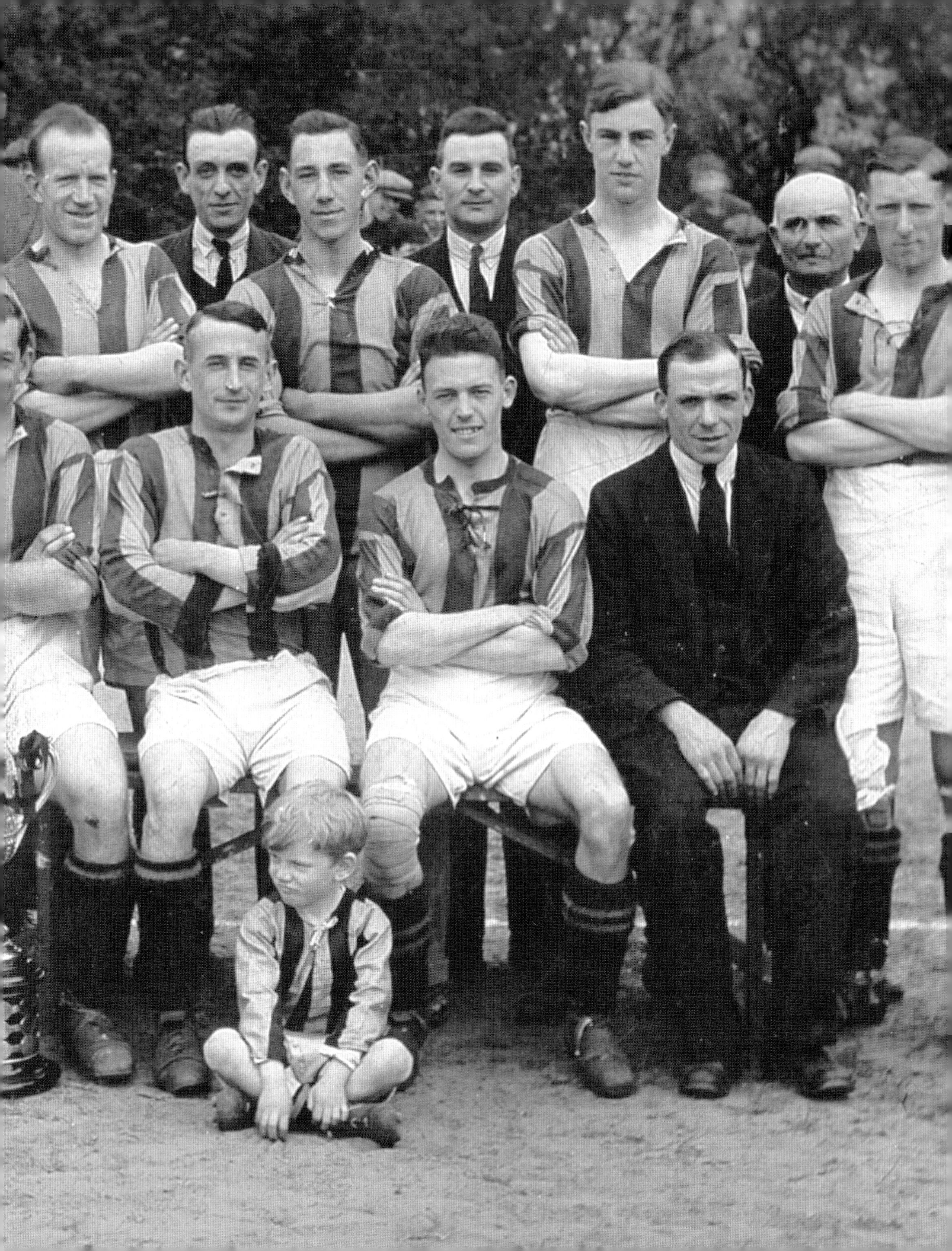

CHESHIRE LEAGUE DAYS

died playing football after he had left Nantwich. Frank Simon, the skipper, had played League football for Port Vale. He joined Nantwich from Winsford United and was later to manage the Three Pigeons pub in the town. They were kept in trim by the trainer - Walter Cooper, a former Nantwich player.

'Yogga' as he was known, had been appointed at the beginning of the season and was still called upon, from time to time, to put his boots on. The last occasion was for an early evening match at Northwich Victoria when he got a knock early on and had to go off (in those days there were no substitutes). He was soon followed by Billy Slight who was concussed in a collision - and then by John Turner, a medical student at the time, who was called upon to attend Slight - leaving just eight Nantwich players remaining on the field of play!

In the Cheshire League, Nantwich finished 18th but the fierce nature of the competition was shown when Ashton National signed Alex Jackson, a full Scottish international, from Chelsea. National, who played at what later became Curzon Ashton's ground before their recent move to the Tameside Stadium, had started out as a works team for the National Gas and Oil Engine Company. Seizing their opportunity to grab the limelight, they shelled out £8000 to sign Johnson in a blaze of publicity. It was an astronomical fee for that era but the Scotsman was happy to sign having been embroiled in a contractual dispute with Chelsea. Sadly, after all the publicity, Johnson's presence didn't have the desired effect on National's performances in the Cheshire League and his contract was eventually cancelled by mutual consent after he sustained an injury on Christmas Eve.

Jackson's appearance at London Road didn't capture the imagination of the Nantwich public. Gate receipts amounted to little over £25 when National came to town in November 1932. And, no, the Scottish international didn't help Ashton to victory - Nantwich won the match 1-0!

CHESHIRE LEAGUE FORTUNES
A chart plotting Nantwich's decline in league positions during the club's first spell in the Cheshire County League from 1919 to 1938.
(Only 12 clubs competed in 1919/20, increasing to 18 then 20, with a full complement of 22 from 1923/24)

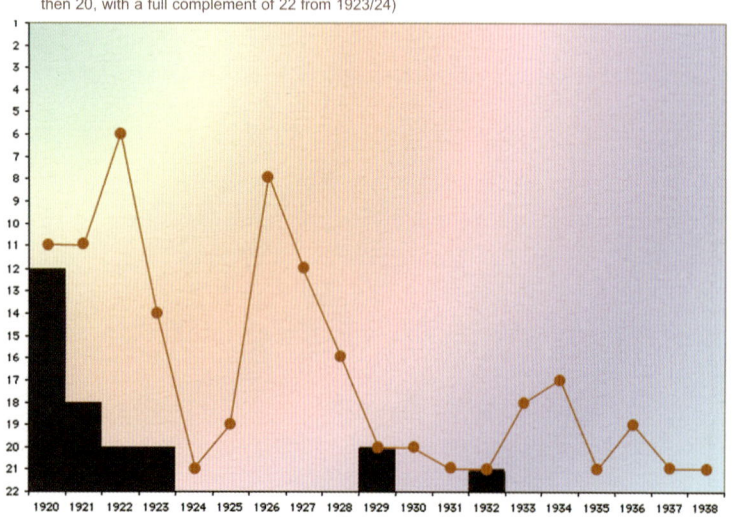

Sadly the success in the Senior Cup failed to spur the club on to greater things. Finances were still tight and, in fact, a loss of £147 was reported despite the winning of the Senior Cup. The inability to pay big wages to bring in better players continued to take its toll on the pitch with the Dabbers taking some hefty beatings on the pitch. In September 1933, Hyde United racked up an 11-0 victory and the following March, double figures were again conceded in a 10-3 defeat at Stalybridge Celtic.

By 1935, the club was in debt to the tune of £400 and, to make matters worse, gales in January 1936 again blew down half the stands.

THE LEAGUE MEN

Nantwich players who have gone on to feature in the Football League

Part 2: Between the wars

George Clarke (1919, Stoke 156 League appearances, 4 goals; Crewe 2)

Frank Birchenough (1919, West Ham 1, Burnley 2)

Jack Thompson (1919, Aston Villa 26; Brighton 94)

Frank Mellor (1920, Bolton 2)

Ted Steventon (1920, Stoke 3)

Herbert Simpson (1921, Bolton 9,1; Wigan Borough 69,7)

Ossie Purcell (1922, Crewe 8,5)

Harry Boston (1923, Bolton 37,2; West Brom 27,6; Swansea 19)

Billy Houston (1925, Crewe 2,1)

Jack Prince (1927, Oldham 1, Port Vale 43, Rochdale 15, Wrexham 3)

Albert Sewell (1927, Crewe 55)

Freddie Worrall (1928, Oldham 105,21; Portsmouth 316,69; Crewe 6,1; England)

Harry O'Grady (1929, Port Vale 1; Southampton 7,2; Leeds 8,2; Burnley 13,8; Bury 15,4; Millwall 4; Carlisle 28,9; Accrington 23,2)

Frank Davies (1930, Northampton 144,7)

John Molloy (1932, Wrexham 1, Halifax 6)

Eric Stubbs (1934, Wrexham 28,10, Nottm Forest 22,6; Leicester 77,15)

Cyrus Johnson (1935, New Brighton 10,6)

Albert Pinxton (1935, Blackburn 3; Cardiff 20,3 Torquay 4)

Tommy Williamson (1935, Oldham 157,4)

George Cope (1936, Crewe 14)

John Essex (1937, Crewe 13, Stockport 43)

Geoffrey Spencer (1938, West Brom 13,2; Brighton 3)

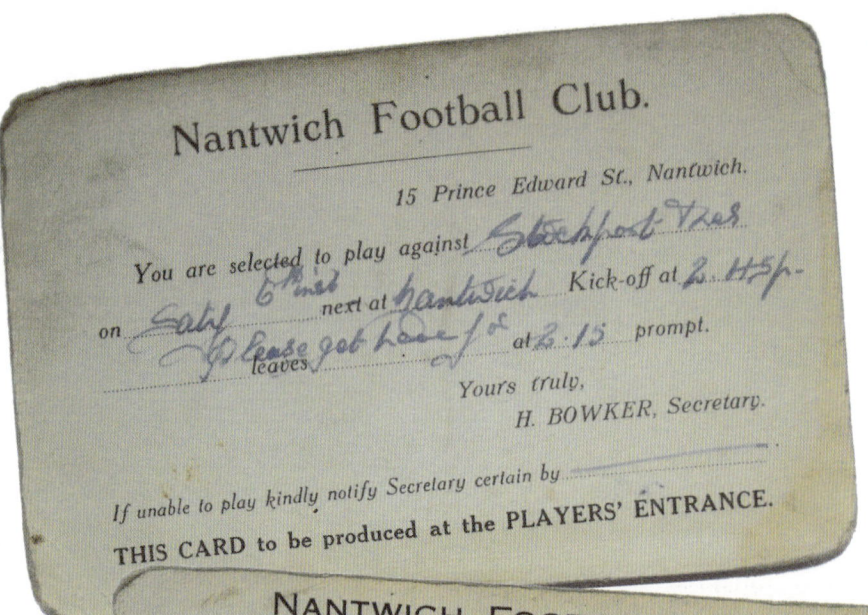

CHESHIRE LEAGUE DAYS

On the pitch, results were going from bad to worse. In September 1936, in the space of three days, Nantwich lost 11-3 at home to Congleton Town and 12-0 at Runcorn. Then, in April 1938, Nantwich visited Prenton Park and returned home with a 13-0 hiding, Ted Buckley netting a sensational TEN goals for Tranmere Rovers Reserves. In pre-floodlight days, Nantwich, it has to be said, were struggling to raise a side for the late afternoon midweek fixture and trainer Billy Gray (who later became club secretary) was called upon to make up the numbers. Runcorn, who were going head-to-head with Tranmere for the league title, put in a complaint - but their appeal wasn't upheld. Rovers went on to clinch the title by three points; Nantwich finished next to bottom in that 1937/38 season. As a result, they were again in a position of having to apply for re-election to the Cheshire League. Debts had now spiralled to over £800 and so, with some regret, the decision was taken to withdraw the application for re-election. After nearly 20 years, the inevitable had happened and financial pressures had sadly forced Nantwich to drop out of the Cheshire League, being replaced by Wellington Town of the Birmingham League.

**SELECTION CARD
v Stockport County Reserves
6 November 1937**
Players were sent postcards advising they had been selected to play for the club. These cards were sent by secretary Harry Bowker to Alfred Lightfoot who made his Nantwich debut in this Cheshire League game. Nantwich lost 3-1 and the former Winsford United player rarely featured afterwards.

Despite dropping down to the Crewe & District Amateur League for the 1938/39 campaign, the Dabbers continued to struggle on the pitch. ICI Alkali gained revenge for the Senior Cup defeat six years earlier by handing out a 10-1 spanking in Nantwich's second league match. Results picked up later in the season so there was much optimism ahead of the 1939/40 campaign.

However, as preparations were made for the new season, the dark clouds of war again gathered over Europe. In early September, Haslington Villa were beaten 6-1 in an FA Cup Preliminary Round tie. It proved to be the club's last game for nearly seven years as bigger battles were set to rage around the world.

The 40s, 50s & 60s

Peace returned to Europe in 1945 and, after the brutalities and devastation of war, a fresh tide of hope and optimism swept across the country. Some football was resumed for the 1945/46 season but most leagues needed a bit of time to get themselves organised again after the chaos of war. So too did Nantwich Football Club.

Thanks to the initiative of Albert Peake (Chairman) and Billy Gray (Secretary), the club got up and running again for the 1946/47 season with former player Ted Steventon taking on the role of President. One of the main difficulties was the lack of a home ground as the old London Road enclosure was unavailable. When war had broken out again in 1939, the ground (then owned by Jacksons the builders) was rented out to Gerald Fox. He used it as a chicken run and kept hens in the dressing rooms – and turkeys in the referee's hut (some would say no change there then !!). When the club started up again in 1946, home games were played firstly at the Grammar School and then on the Barony with teams changing in the nearby Baronia Works. The club was grateful to the old Nantwich Urban Council for allowing the use of the Barony and a post and wire fence was put up around the pitch. However, the bad condition of the pitches saw many games called off (one home game was even played on the King George V playing fields in Crewe).

Post war restrictions meant it was impossible to secure a black and amber kit as had been worn before the war. Local outfitters Densems offered a full strip with

CLUB BADGE
The old club badge which was sewn onto players' jerseys from after the war right through to the late 1970s

**LES FOXLEY
1946/47**
Took over from goalkeeper Johnny Middleton as Nantwich captain in November 1946, during the first season after the war.

THE 40s, 50s & 60s

white jerseys which was gratefully received by the Committee - though it later turned out that only the socks were meant as a donation!

Nantwich entered the Crewe & District Amateur Combination with former player Andy Blake as trainer and Les Foxley, who later ran a shoe repair shop in Hospital Street, becoming club captain. With rationing still in force and players gradually being de-mobbed, the immediate post-war era still presented difficulties. There was also a mismatch of teams with stronger teams racking up rugby scores against weaker opposition. On one day, Wheelock Albion beat Crewe Co-operative 20-0 whilst Whitchurch Alport hammered Crewe Celtic 22-0. During the season, the Dabbers recorded a 15-1 victory against Audlem Town and won 14-1 at Rolls Royce, which remains the first team's biggest ever away win.

In the FA Cup, Ellesmere Port Town proved much too strong. Captained by former England international 'Pongo' Waring, Port ran out 9-0 winners with the former Villa striker grabbing a hat-trick.

After the hardships of wartime, it seems cruel that the winter of the first post-war footballing season proved so harsh. The arctic winter extended into April with match after match falling victim to snow and ice. The league had to be flexible - and they were. When a Nantwich cup tie at Ruyton fell victim to the weather in the morning, a league game against Rolls Royce was hastily arranged for the afternoon. In an effort to make the Barony Park pitch playable, 20 tons of sand were tipped on it and spread out by eager fans whilst salt was brought in to melt blocks of ice. Match on - and on a mudbath of a pitch Nantwich won 2-0.

Postponed matches and lengthy cup runs saw Nantwich fall behind in their league fixtures. With games in hand, they were catching up with leaders Wheelock Albion but league games continued well into June. By June 2nd, Nantwich needed just a point from their penultimate game against title rivals Wheelock to clinch the title. The weather had now switched from arctic to saharan and the game was played at the old Sandbach Ramblers ground on a baking hot day. "The weather was too hot even for walking," reported the local paper but Nantwich withstood the heat and gained the point they needed in a 1-1 draw.

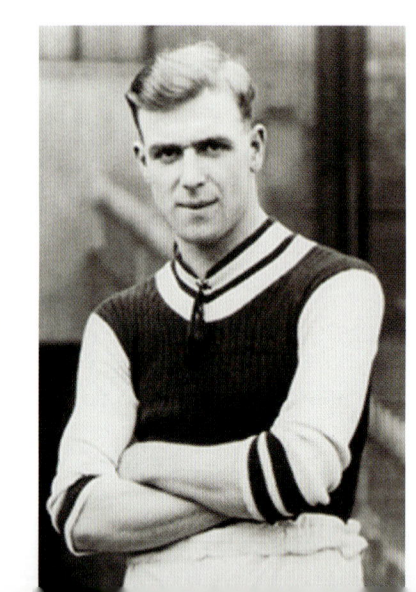

"Never mind the weather, he must see Nantwich"

**ELLESMERE PORT TOWN 9
NANTWICH 0
FA Cup 1st Qualifying Round
21 September 1946**

The back page of the match programme suggests that not even heavy rain was going to stop 'Port fans getting to this eagerly anticipated Cup tie. Those who did would have enjoyed the heavy win over a Nantwich side playing one of its first post-war matches. Former England international Tom 'Pongo' Waring (right) netted a hat-trick.

click4more

More about the career of Pongo Waring is available on-line.
Visit:
www.avfc.premiumtv.co.uk/page/VillaLegendsDetails/0,,10265~1130172,00.html

56

THE 40s, 50s & 60s

NANTWICH FC - 1946/47
An early post-war team photo with Billy Gray (Secretary) standing on the left and Andy Blake (Trainer) standing on the right alongside Chairman Albert Peake. Free-scoring Bobbie Jones is centre of the middle row in front of goalkeeper Johnny Middleton. Presumably Geoff Bull removed his spectacles before playing.

Ten days later, the final match of an eventful season took place with Nantwich beating Crewe Corinthians 5-3. A crowd of almost 1000 assembled to watch the Dabbers be crowned Champions - just nine days ahead of mid-summer.

"The Barony roar was at its loudest when captain Les Foxley stepped up to the farm-cart platform to receive the Crewe Combination trophy from Mr James Batty, Assistant Secretary of the Cheshire FA," said the Crewe Chronicle. Afterwards, there was a celebration at The Railway Hotel for players and officials of the club and the Nantwich Urban Council. "A large iced cake bearing the words 'Nantwich Football Club' and surmounted by a small silver cup was cut and distributed among the company."

The club also enjoyed an eventful run in the Commander Ethelston Cup. Entering at the second round, Nantwich were leading Crewe LMS 3-0 when the match had to be adandoned with 20 minutes remaining when Lewis, the LMS centre forward, steamed into the Nantwich goalposts breaking them beyond hope of repair! When the match was replayed, Bobbie Jones netted the only goal to secure a Third Round tie away to Ruyton-XI-Towns.

57

The Colourful World of Nantwich Football Club

Over the years, Nantwich players have pulled on virtually every colour under the sun. Almost every permutation of reds, blues, maroons, claret, amber, black and white has been in evidence – as well as present day green, of course.

Add to this rainbow of colours, a dash of stripes, hoops and quarters and you have the veritable cocktail of kits the Dabbers have sported over a century and a quarter.

Back in 1884, the newly-formed club started out wearing scarlet stripes. Kits were changed fairly frequently in those days and by the time Nantwich entered the Shropshire & District League for the 1891/92 campaign, the old 'Crewe & Nantwich Advertiser' reported that the team was "dressed in blue trousers and blue and white striped shirts".

Around the turn of the century, red was adopted again as the club colours. With maroon and claret variations, it remained so until around 1930. For some reason, there was a major change to

1884

1890s

1900s

1930s

1920s

1938-39

1946-47

1958-59

1959-60

1963-64

black and amber stripes and, bedecked in these colours, Nantwich lifted the coveted Cheshire Senior Cup in 1933.

With black and amber shirts unavailable due to post war restrictions, the club was supplied with white jerseys by local outfitters Densems. However, in 1959, white gave way to red again and it was in these colours that Nantwich re-joined the Cheshire League in 1968.

For the 1971/72 season, a bold move was taken to switch to green – a somewhat uncommon colour for football shirts. It paid dividends with the club capturing the Cheshire Senior Cup for a second time in 1976. The modern vogue for changing strips virtually every year saw a variation of green shades and strips worn in the late 80s and early 90s.

In 1995/96, a change was made to black and white stripes but it was to be short-lived. By 2002/03, Nantwich were back wearing the green that is familiar to fans of today, and it was in these colours that the club enjoyed the crowning glory of winning the FA Vase in 2006.

2005-06

2003-05

2001-02

1975-76

1971-72

1984-85

1990-91

1995-96

THE 40s, 50s & 60s

The adverse winter weather had caused the game to be called off three times before it eventually went ahead on April 2nd. Even then, four Ruyton players and Nantwich's Frankie Wright had to leave the field as they couldn't cope with the bitter cold, snow and hail that wreaked havoc during the match. Finally, with 5 minutes still remaining and Nantwich 3-0 up, Ruyton conceded the match.

In the semi-finals, there was a thrilling victory over Crewe Corinthians. A late penalty by Tommy Hope levelled the scores up at 5-5 and took the tie into extra time. The Dabbers went into overdrive, cruising to an 11-5 win and setting up a Final against Wem Town 'B' at Whitchurch. Bobbie Jones scored a whooping 60 goals that season but he failed to turn up for training in the run up to the Final and so his place was given to Tommy Brassington. Without their talismanic marksman, Nantwich stuttered and although Brassington scored, Wem ran out 3-1 winners.

The success on the pitch encouraged developments behind the scenes. Jim Wainwright, Harold Clarke and Eric Fleet were amongst those who joined the Committee with the trio going on to put in unstinting service to the club over many years, each being made a Life Member. For once, the club was in the black (by £70) and a financial secretary was appointed to oversee finances. The team was still picked by a selection committee but former player Tom Nicholls was made trainer-coach.

The following season, the Dabbers slipped to third in the league and suffered another hefty defeat in the FA Cup - crashing 8-1 at Altrincham in the Preliminary Round.

The club, though, was becoming more forward-thinking. Plans were hatched to secure the club's future by purchasing the London Road ground. As full members of the Football Association, the club was able to secure a loan of £750 from the FA and buy the ground. However, despite now owning the ground, the club still had difficulties getting Mr Fox off the land as it was considered to be agricultural. As a result, Committee men had to sweep part of the ground before each match to remove hen and geese droppings. Fox's poultry continued to encroach onto the pitch and, on one occasion Mr Fox, later a good supporter of the club, drove his lorry across the pitch whilst a match was in progress! With the dressing rooms occupied by hens and geese, the teams had to change in the Bull's Head bowling green pavilion which stood opposite The Leopard in London Road.

Even after normality returned after the war, Mr Fox was allowed to keep sheep on the playing pitch - it saved having to get the grass cut! On match days the sheep would be taken off and marched down the road to be put in a pen at the Bull's Head. Before kick off, the Committee used to clean as much sheep muck as possible off the pitch. Pity those defenders who made a sliding tackle only to find a pile had been missed !!

FRED EVERALL
A new signing for the start of the 1947/48 season in the Crewe & District Amateur League. A half-back, Fred was previously with Crewe Alexandra's 'A' side.

THE 40s, 50s & 60s

The club also stepped up its level of football and became founder members of the Mid-Cheshire League in 1948. Centre forward Dennis Thornhill was signed from Crewe Alexandra but it proved to be the goals from Jimmy Cooke that the team relied on. Cooke finished top scorer with 25 goals as Nantwich finished 7th in the table. One of Cooke's goals was in the Final of the Mid-Cheshire League Cup against Runcorn Athletic. Nantwich lost the match 2-1 and their disappointment was compounded when they found out that no medals were handed out to the losing finalists.

The 1949/50 season started in disappointing fashion. Despite a goal from former Crewe LMS forward Geoff White, Nantwich suffered a crushing 10-1 defeat at Droylsden United in the FA Cup Preliminary Round. Between the sticks that afternoon was Harold Jones who served the club for three seasons. After the final whistle, the Droylsden manager gathered his players round to clap the keeper off the pitch. "What are you clapping me off for?" Harold asked. "Well, if it hadn't have been for you the score would have been 30-1," came the reply!

Things started to pick up, though, after the new decade was ushered in. After the ravages of wartime, the 50s would see the country return to 'normality'. The launch of the 'Top 20' in 1952 led to an explosion in popular music with the nation set to be swept away on a tide of rock 'n roll.

The new decade had hardly begun when Nantwich's first and second teams rock 'n rolled on the same day, netting 20 goals on 28th January 1950. The first team won their Mid-Cheshire League game at Goostrey 8-0. Alan Cooke notched a six minute hat-trick on his way to going nap whilst Denis Nicholls (2) and Brian Dutton completed the rout. Meanwhile, back at base, the reserves weren't to be outdone, hammering Holmes Chapel 12-0 with Jack Young helping himself to four goals.

The Dabbers finished Mid-Cheshire League runners-up the following season but the 50s was generally a period of post-war consolidation.

NANTWICH v FODENS
Cheshire Senior Cup
24 September 1949
Nantwich keeper Harold Jones thwarts two Fodens attacks in this 1st Qualifying Round tie. Goals from Alan Cooke, Jimmy Cooke, Denis Nicholls (2) and Alan Western secured a 5-2 win.

POST-WAR ST★RS

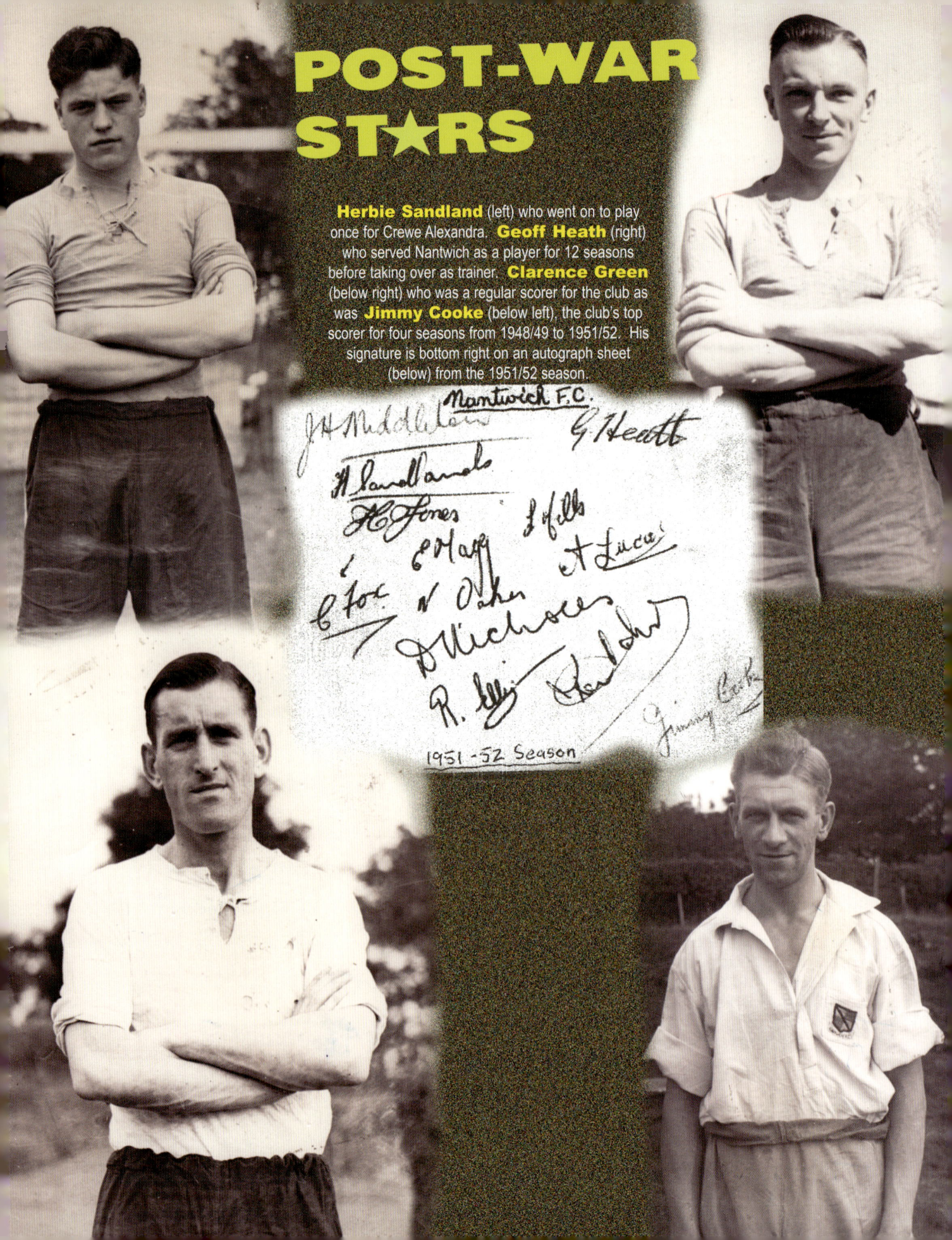

Herbie Sandland (left) who went on to play once for Crewe Alexandra. **Geoff Heath** (right) who served Nantwich as a player for 12 seasons before taking over as trainer. **Clarence Green** (below right) who was a regular scorer for the club as was **Jimmy Cooke** (below left), the club's top scorer for four seasons from 1948/49 to 1951/52. His signature is bottom right on an autograph sheet (below) from the 1951/52 season.

THE **40s, 50s & 60s**

There was, however, quite a distraction when Nantwich's youth team were drawn against mighty Manchester United in the the inaugural season of the FA Youth Cup. The Football Association had decided to instigate the competition as a means of encouraging clubs to develop young players. In that first season (1952/53) entry to the tournament was restricted to clubs who were full members of the FA.

Having received a bye in the First Round, Nantwich were drawn at home to the formidable 'Busby Babes' in the Second Round. Matt Busby offered the club £50 for the venue to be switched to United's training ground - The Cliff at Broughton. Nantwich agreed so the match took place on 4th November 1952 under primitive floodlighting of ten poles down each side of the ground with one light on each.

On the night, the Nantwich team bus was late getting to the venue. Heading into Manchester on the Chester Road, the driver spotted floodlights in the distance and headed towards them - only to end up at the White City greyhound stadium!

Perhaps it was an omen of what was in store for the young Dabbers that night! United lent Nantwich flourescent yellow shirts which would show up better under the lights and to help players and spectators alike, an orange ball was also used. In fact, there were two orange balls. Heavy rain throughout the day had made the pitch so muddy that one ball was washed off whilst the other was in play!

A crowd of 2600 flocked to see United's young magicians take on the no-hopers from little Nantwich. The great Duncan Edwards was in United's line-up as were David Pegg, Albert Scanlon and Ronnie Cope - names that were all to become Old Trafford legends. Sadly for the kids from South Cheshire, there was to be no fairy tale ending. It took just three minutes for Pegg to open the scoring and after 6 minutes it was already 3-0. The match was hopelessly one sided and, from his wing-half position Edwards went on to score five times as United chalked up a rugby score. 10-0 at half-time, United coach Jimmy Murphy demanded more of his young guns in the second half. He wasn't to be disappointed! The final result of 23-0 remains a record for the competition which is unlikely ever to be beaten. Pegg and John Doherty also scored five each whilst Eddie Lewis had to be content with just four. Just for good measure, the young Red Devils also rattled the woodwork four times! Remarkably, Matt Busby was so impressed by Nantwich keeper Brian Thorley that he signed him on. Brian went on to play for United's junior sides on several occasions without breaking into the first team squad. Thorley's counterpart in

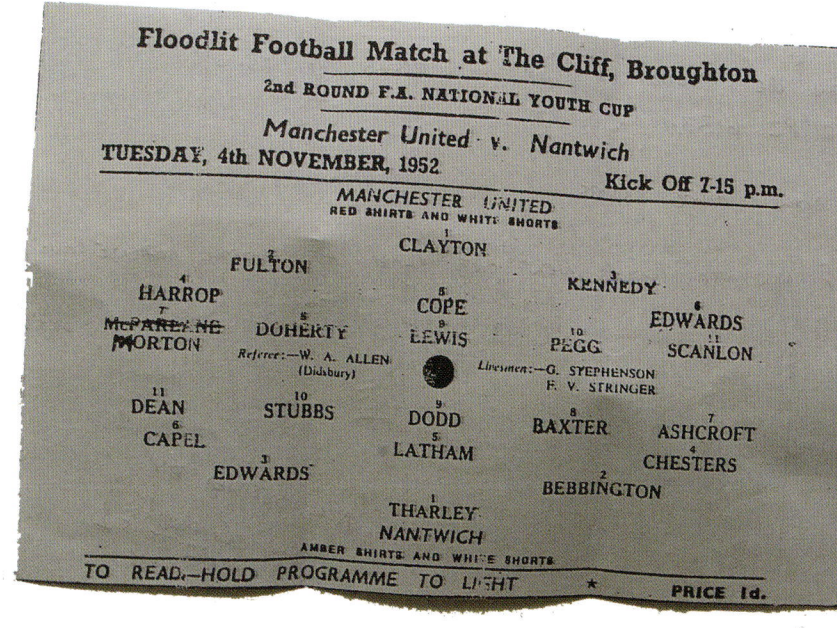

NANTWICH 0
MANCHESTER UNITED 23
FA Youth Cup
4 November 1952
Official Programme
Line-ups for the match played at The Cliff, Broughton were:
Nantwich: Brian Thorley, Ken Bebbington, Ernie Edwards, Colin Chesters, Don Latham, Maurice Capel, Maurice Ashcroft, Gordon Baxter, Brian Dodd, Frank Stubbs, John Dean.
Manchester United: Gordon Clayton, Bryce Fulton, Paddy Kennedy, Bobby Harrop, Ronnie Cope, Duncan Edwards, Alan Morton, John Doherty, Eddie Lewis, David Pegg, Albert Scanlon.
Scorers: Doherty (5), D Edwards (5), E Edwards og, Lewis (4), Morton (2), Pegg (5), Scanlon
Attendance:2600
Receipts:£216

63

THE 40s, 50s & 60s

click4more
Watch a video clip of Sir Matt Busby and Sir Bobby Charlton profiling the legendary Duncan Edwards.
Visit:
www.youtube.com/watch?v=ADOqaqXjbDk

RONNIE COPE
Manchester United
(born Crewe, 5 October 1934)
England Schoolboys,
Manchester United, Luton Town,
Northwich Victoria, Winsford
United & Nantwich Town.

the United goal, Gordon Clayton was a virtual spectator - touching the ball less than ten times in the whole game!

However, despite the hefty rout, Nantwich sportingly gave Ronnie Cope a lift back to his Crewe home on the team bus. Ronnie was a 16 year old Crewe lad whose father George, a hefty well-built man, had played regularly with Nantwich before the war, going on to sign for the Alex and having trials with Manchester City. After breaking through into the first team, Ronnie chalked up over 100 United appearances, ironically going on to finish his career with Nantwich after stints at Luton Town, Northwich Victoria and Winsford United.

The match is well remembered by Ronnie. "They gave us fluorescent jerseys to wear. Not like a football shirt at all – more like a workman wears on site! The match was unbelievable really. Every time we went down we scored. Almost everyone scored that day apart from the goalkeeper and me! I reckon it was the best youth team that United ever had." And what of the mercurial Duncan Edwards? "Duncan was one hell of a skilful player, and well built for his age, too. He was a lovely lad – yes, a smashing lad. A fantastic player, of course, one of the best ever to play for England even at his tender age."

And did he enjoy that lift back on the Nantwich team coach? "Billy Gray was in charge of the Nantwich team at the time. I asked Billy if I could have a lift back on their team bus as I still lived in Crewe. 'No you damn well can't,' was his initial response – though he did let me on in the end."

United went on to win the Youth Cup (beating Wolves 9-3 in a two-legged final) that year - and for the next four seasons! Still only 16, Edwards became the youngest footballer to play in England's top flight when he made his full United debut less than 5 months later. Edwards was capped 18 times for England before losing his life at the tender age of 21 in that tragic fateful winter night in Munich.

The story is also told that in the late sixties, Billy Gray and his guest, Frank Bickerton, went to see a game at Old Trafford on a Cheshire FA executive visit. There, they both met Matt Busby who was master-minding United to European Cup glory. On hearing they had come from Nantwich, Busby, who was known for having a fantastic memory, remarked, "Nantwich, Nantwich, let me see ... Oh yes, I remember - we beat them 23-0 in the FA Youth Cup in 1952, but everybody at the club was very friendly and kind to us."

Many of that Nantwich Youth team progressed to play for the senior side with John Dean's 14 goals making him top scorer the following season as Nantwich finished 12th in the Mid-Cheshire League. The team struggled to challenge for honours throughout the 50s despite some well known local players pulling on the shirt. Veteran Ernie Tagg (later Crewe Alex's Manager) turned out for the club, as did Herbert Sandland (who made a single first team appearance for the Alex

If anyone can claim to be Nantwich's biggest fan, it has to be Jim Kettle. Born in February 1920, Jim has been following his beloved Dabbers since he was a nine year old lad. Back then, he would nip out of his house, pop round the corner and watch his schoolboy heroes taking on the finest footballers in the area as Nantwich took on the best in the old Cheshire League.

"I would say in all my years of watching Nantwich, the finest team was that back in the 30s," Jim fondly remembers. "There was Cyrus Johnson at centre forward – a huge guy and always smiling. Billy Slight – he was a great player. It was often said that he could easily have played football professionally for a League club, but he didn't want to – he had a good job! At left back was Vic Fox. He was a decent cricketer and played for Nantwich Cricket Club so always missed the first few games because of the overlap with the football and cricket seasons."

1933 - and Nantwich won the Cheshire Senior Cup for the first time. Sadly for young Jim, the final was at Northwich. "My parents wouldn't let me travel to away games so I missed the match. My Dad was never really interested in football." But if Jim hasn't inherited the Nantwich football bug, he's certainly passed it on. Four generations of Kettles are now on the boil at the Weaver Stadium which echoes to the matchday drumming of grandson Peter. Son Graham served on the club Committee for many years and, amongst other things, Graham helped set up the social club at the old ground. He was even named on the bench once when 80s Manager Cliff Hodgkinson was short on numbers! Great grandsons Sam and Josh are the young Dabbers who make up Nantwich's number one football family.

And Jim's best Nantwich player of all time? "Slight was a fantastic player, so too was Frank Simon – a big, bald chap who kept the Three Pigeons pub." But the best ever?? "Harry Boston. He'd been a regular in Bolton's first team and would just walk around the pitch. Some people didn't like it. Players would be belting around everywhere, sweat dripping off them but Harry would take it all at a stroll. He didn't need to run everywhere like everyone else, he was such a class player."

GENTLEMAN JIM

Over the years, Jim served on the Committee, painted goal posts, ran raffles, cleaned dressing rooms and worked on the pitch at Jackson Avenue. In 2008, he was named William Hill Fan of the Year at the National Game Awards.

Accompanied by Peter, Jim proudly collected his award at a glitzy presentation at Arsenal's plush Emirates Stadium – deserved recognition for his years of dedication to the club.

FAMILY AFFAIR Jim with his Fan Of The Year award, surrounded by son Graham, grandson Pete and great grandsons Sam and Josh.

THE 40s, 50s & 60s

after Ralph Ward signed him on as an amateur), John Davies (who became a solicitor and later on club President) and, of course, Geoff Heath who was a regular in the side for many years before becoming trainer first at Nantwich then at Stoke City and Crewe Alex.

In opposition ranks, there was also a name that would become well known to the wider world. A raw youngster by the name of Roger Hunt netted twice for Stockton Heath when they came to Nantwich and poached a 3-2 victory in the Mid-Cheshire League during the 1955/56 season. How many of the spectators dotted around the old London Road ground that day could have guessed that the 17 year old would become a World Cup winner with England some ten years later? Ironically, the Stockton Heath side was managed at the time by Freddie Worrall the former Nantwich player who, himself, had gone on to play for England.

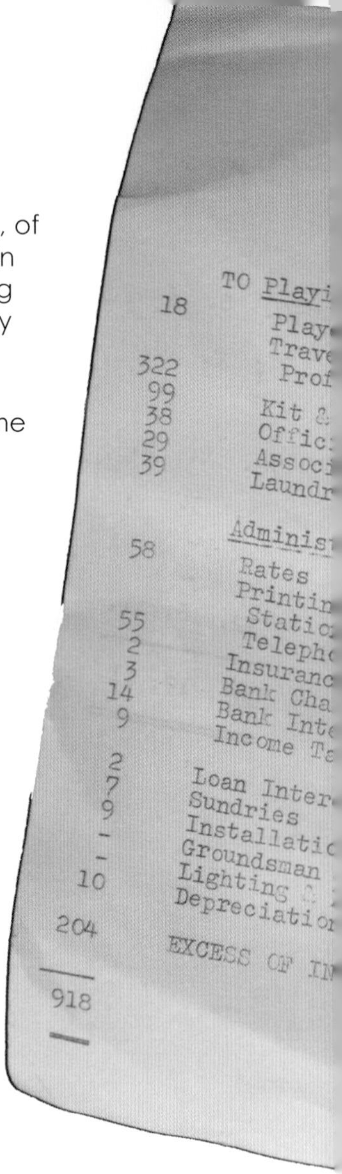

There were, during the late 50s, some heavy defeats though - 11-1 at Barnton (54/55), 10-2 at Stockton Heath (56/57) and 9-1 at Knutsford (58/59). By the time that conscription (or National Service as it had come to be known) was formally ended in 1960, a new partnership was beginning to be formed behind the scenes that would prove to be the springboard for success on the pitch. In 1959, Jack Lindop took over from Reg Kent as club Secretary and soon afterwards Eddie Lockyer became Chairman when local butcher and former player Arthur Broomhall stepped down.

Stability is the key to success in football. Ask followers of Manchester United or Arsenal and they will soon tell you the success of their great clubs in recent times is built on the spadework put in by Sir Alex Ferguson and Arsene Wenger over many seasons. For many years, Jack Lindop and Eddie Lockyer gave Nantwich that stability.

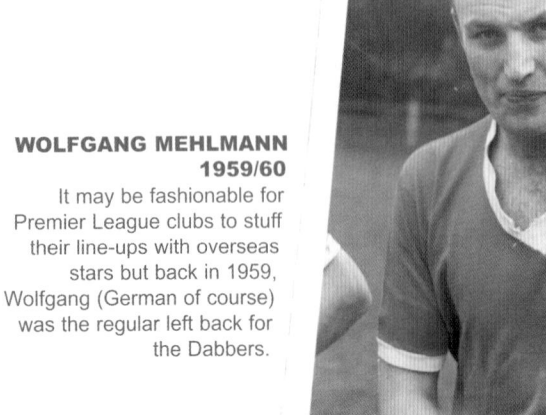

ARTHUR COOPER
1958/59
Pictured outside the old changing rooms at the London Road ground, painted in distinctive black and white stripes. Over zealous washing of the kit saw the black quarters on the jerseys fade to grey by the end of the campaign.

WOLFGANG MEHLMANN
1959/60
It may be fashionable for Premier League clubs to stuff their line-ups with overseas stars but back in 1959, Wolfgang (German of course) was the regular left back for the Dabbers.

66

THE 40s, 50s & 60s

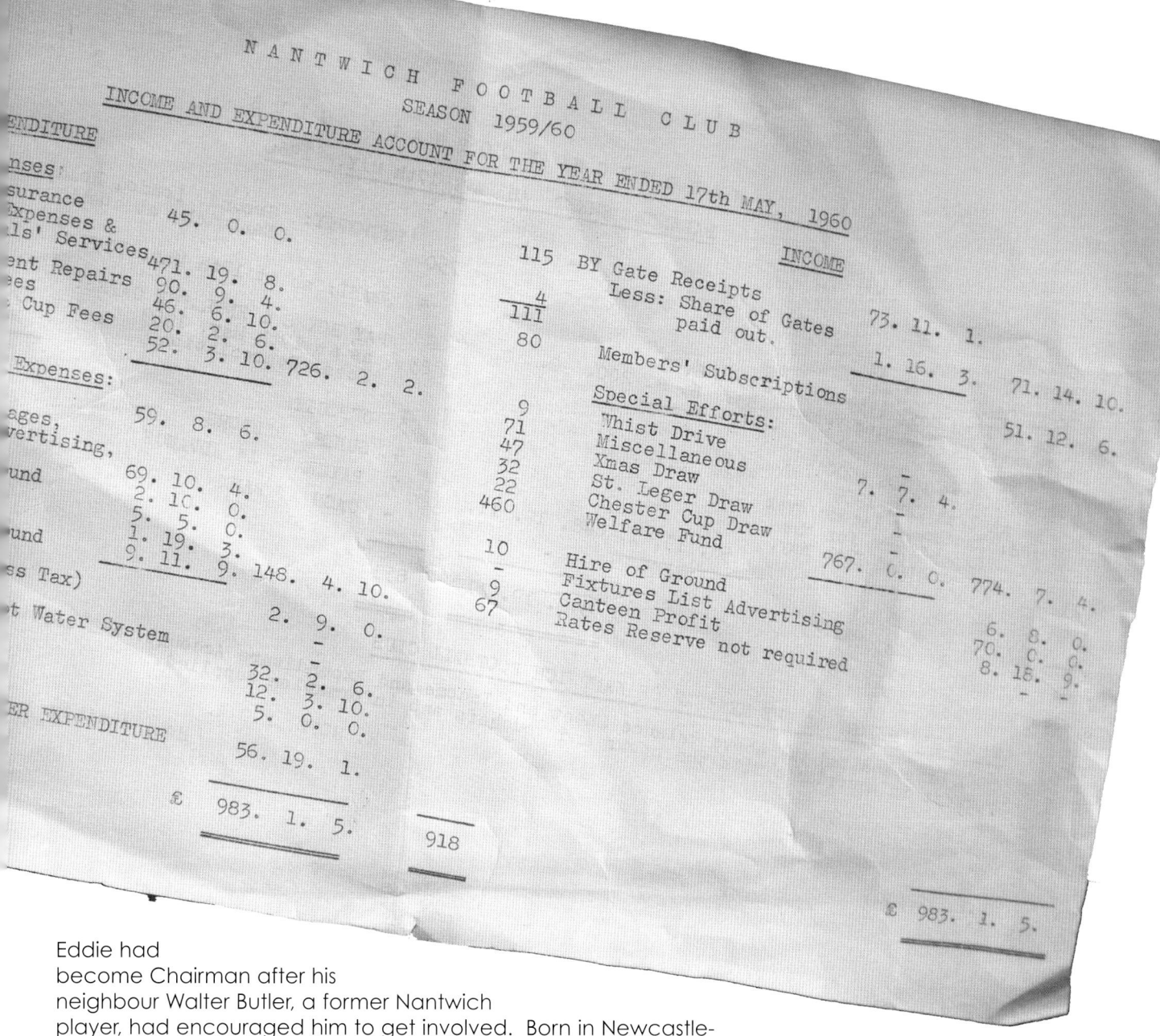

NANTWICH FOOTBALL CLUB
SEASON 1959/60
INCOME AND EXPENDITURE ACCOUNT FOR THE YEAR ENDED 17th MAY, 1960

[Account document – partially obscured on left edge]

EXPENDITURE

Item	£ s. d.		Item	£ s. d.
...nses:				
...surance	45. 0. 0.			
...xpenses & ...ls' Services	471. 19. 8.			
...nt Repairs	90. 9. 4.			
...es	46. 6. 10.			
...Cup Fees	20. 2. 6.			
	52. 3. 10.	726. 2. 2.		
...Expenses:				
...ages,	59. 8. 6.			
...vertising,	69. 10. 4.			
...und	2. 10. 0.			
	5. 5. 0.			
...und	1. 19. 3.			
(...ss Tax)	9. 11. 9.	148. 4. 10.		
...t Water System		2. 9. 0.		
	32. 2. 6.			
	12. 3. 10.			
	5. 0. 0.			
...ER EXPENDITURE		56. 19. 1.		
	£	983. 1. 5.		

INCOME

Item	£ s. d.	£ s. d.
BY Gate Receipts	115	
Less: Share of Gates paid out.	4	
	111	73. 11. 1.
	80	
Members' Subscriptions		1. 16. 3.
Special Efforts:		71. 14. 10.
Whist Drive	9	
Miscellaneous	71	51. 12. 6.
Xmas Draw	47	
St. Leger Draw	32	
Chester Cup Draw	22	7. 7. 4.
Welfare Fund	460	
Hire of Ground	10	767. 0. 0.
Fixtures List Advertising	9	774. 7. 4.
Canteen Profit	67	6. 8. 0.
Rates Reserve not required		70. 0. 0.
		8. 18. 9.
	918	
	£	983. 1. 5.

Eddie had become Chairman after his neighbour Walter Butler, a former Nantwich player, had encouraged him to get involved. Born in Newcastle-under-Lyme, Eddie had trained as an architect before serving in the army. During the war he had been wounded by shrapnel in Syracuse, Sicily but, when peace returned, he became an architect of post-war housing in Nantwich. Sadly, the war wounds led to Eddie losing his sight in 1950 but he retrained as a telephone operator under the Royal National Institute for the Blind. He remained, though, very active in pursuing his interests. A Vice-President of Crewe & District FA, he also served as President and Chairman of the Nantwich branch of NALGO and was an official of the Nantwich Amateur Boxing Club and Nantwich Entertainments Association.

It was the football club, though, that was Eddie's main passion and, in some ways, he believed his disability helped him during his 18 years

CLUB ACCOUNTS 1959/60
The club's reliance on its Welfare Fund is readily apparent.

The cliche 'scoring goals for fun' could well have been made for **Gerry Duffy**. Wherever he played, you could be sure he'd find the back of the net. His prolific career included two spells with Nantwich, a couple of seasons in the League with Oldham Athletic and a remarkable sojourn into European club football with the now-defunct Welsh side Borough United.

Gerry first came to prominence with **Northwich Victoria**. He made his Cheshire League debut late in the 1953/54 season, grabbing his first goal in the final match of the season against Hyde United. He then served **Witton Albion** and **Middlewich Athletic** and is reputed to have scored over 100 goals for Middlewich in 1955/56 - paving the way for him signing for **Oldham Athletic** in May 1956.

The man from Middlewich scored a goal every other game for the Latics during their 1957/58 campaign in the old Third Division North but departed the following season having netted 21 goals in 58 appearances for the Boundary Park club.

Starring for **Nantwich** in 1961/62 he included a four goal haul in the 5-0 home win over Runcorn Athletic as he topped the Dabbers' goal chart. His goal in the 3-1 win over ICI Alkali in the Mid-Cheshire League Cup Final, helped put senior silverware in the Nantwich trophy cabinet for the first time in nearly three decades.

Next stop on the goal run was now-defunct Welsh side **Borough United**, scoring 38 goals in 1962/63 helping them to the Welsh League (North) title and to lift the Welsh Cup. The following season, he took part in Borough's European Cup Winners' Cup adventure. Drawn against Sliema Wanderers of Malta, the United party took a draining 31 hours to reach the Med for the first leg. Their plane had to dramatically divert to Marseille because of engine trouble – and they took to the pitch just four hours after arriving, a request for postponement having been refused. The match took place at the national stadium in Gzira, before 15,000 spectators, and in the circumstances Borough did well to hold out for a 0-0 draw on an unfamiliar sandy surface.

Borough's ground in Llandudno Junction wasn't fit to host the second leg so the tie was played at Wrexham - in front of a crowd of over 17,000 !! The Maltese struggled somewhat on an unfamiliar grass surface, and a goal in each half, (Duffy, of course, got one), sent United through. Sadly, the odyssey ended with a 4-0 aggregate defeat to Slovan Bratislava in the Second Round.

After three seasons in the Welsh League, the Goal Machine re-joined **Nantwich**. Unsurprisingly, he scored twice on his return in a 8-1 trouncing of Hyde United Reserves in the Manchester League in January 1966. This time however Duffy, who also enjoyed spells with **Colwyn Bay** and **Winsford United**, didn't stay long at London Road - but long enough to take his tally of Nantwich goals over the half-century mark!

GERRY DUFFY

Birthplace Middlewich
Birthdate 9 September 1934
Nantwich Career
1961/62 Mid Cheshire League 43 goals (39 League, 4 Cups)
1965/66 Manchester League 9 goals (7 League, 2 Cups)

click4more
Watch a video clip of Gerry Duffy and his Borough United teammates from the 1963 Welsh Cup winning side at a players' reunion in 1994. Visit: www.youtube.com/watch?gl=GB&v=Cy-QFBACDkU

THE 40s, 50s & 60s

as Chairman. He once commented, "In a way, it helped to be blind, for you have to be a good listener and so I was always able to work on a concensus of opinion." Eddie used to like to get to the matches early "to soak up the atmosphere" and then, on a Sunday morning, he would listen to a tape recording of the game made for him by Peter Partridge who worked in Crewe Works.

With Eddie and Jack being backed by an enthusiastic Committee, steps were taken to improve the club's London Road ground and, for the first time a Manager was appointed - Alan Martin, the former Port Vale and Stoke City inside forward. With Martin as player-manager, Nantwich finished Mid-Cheshire League runners-up to Middlewich Athletic in 1961/62 and won the Mid-Cheshire League Cup. The Dabbers needed extra time to overcome old foes ICI Alkali 3-1 in the Final, lifting the trophy for the first time after 13 years of membership of the Mid-Cheshire League. There was also a run to the Final of the Cheshire Amateur Cup but Lostock Gralam came out 2-0 winners in a replay at the Barton Stadium, Winsford.

OPENING OF NEW CHANGING ROOMS
November 1960
Jack Parker, President of the Cheshire FA, presides over the opening ceremony. Lined up behind him are Eddie Lockyer (Chairman), Bob Lomas (Treasurer), Billy Gray, Peter Wilson (President), Joe Blagg (Chairman, Nantwich Urban District Council), Harold Owen, Arthur Broomhall and Frank Foden.

ALAN MARTIN
August 1961
Secretary Jack Lindop (left) and Chairman Eddie Lockyer (right) secure the signature of Nantwich's first player-manager.

NANTWICH RESERVES 1961/62
Crewe & District FA Cup winners
Standing (Left to right): Neville Clarke (Trainer), Derek Betteley, Billy Haddock, Ken Nixon, Billy Gray, Jim Barfoot, Roger Mason, Jackie Hodgkinson, Eddie Lockyer (Chairman), Vin Phipps.
Kneeling: Dave Brown, Peter Noden, Dave Poole, Jim Wheatley, Ken Jones.

69

THE 40s, 50s & 60s

MISS NANTWICH TOWN FC 1963
Sheila Knowles
Miss Knowles is crowned by Joe Blagg (Chairman, Nantwich UDC) alongside Eddie Lockyer and (front) Keith Williamson.

Alan Martin was succeeded by the ambitious appointment of Alan Ball senior for the 1962/63 campaign. Nantwich slipped to third in the table but the foundations were laid for a record-breaking 1963/64 campaign. The former Southport forward led Nantwich to a remarkable 'treble', clinching the Mid-Cheshire League championship having lost just two league matches all season.

Ball brought in Alan Groves from ICI Alkali to be his captain. 'Satch', as he was nicknamed, was a foraging wing forward and was a huge influence on the field. He served Nantwich for five seasons but a couple of years after leaving the club suffered a heart attack from which he sadly died in December 1969.

Sharpshooters in Ball's line-up were Micky Brookes and Jimmy Fletcher who both notched 18 league goals as the Dabbers finished five points ahead of runners-up Lostock Gralam. Lostock were also beaten 6-0 in the semi-finals of the Mid-Cheshire League Cup which Nantwich lifted after defeating Linotype 3-0 in the Final.

THIS IS THE MATCH NANTWICH WANT TO WIN...

Can get their name on the Cheshire Amateur Cup for the first time in their history

AND SANDBACH SHOULD NOT THWART THEM

THE BATTLE for the League championship over (the team settled that last week at Barnton), Nantwich go into the second stage of their "triple" bid this Saturday, when they meet Sandbach in the final of the Cheshire Amateur Cup on Witton Albion's ground.

Peke's double honour at dog show

NANTWICH SPORTS EDITOR'S DIARY
Nantwich land first league title : Still in with chance of big "treble" : Vine (Shavington) darts winners

NANTWICH CLINCH THE LEAGUE CHAMPIONSHIP
Barnton 1 — Nantwich 3

Nantwich L.V. Darts League champions

ENGLAND EXPECTS

February 1967. England were World Champions, we were in the midst of the swinging sixties and The Monkees were top of the hit parade with I'm A Believer. Things couldn't get any better, could they?? Well, they did for local lad Bert Hulse. The 16 year old was scoring goals for fun in Nantwich's youth team and got the call up for the England youth side. Yes, England.

It seems remarkable in today's era of Premier League Academies and multi-million pound teenagers that a Nantwich player could be selected to wear the Three Lions. But so it was.

Current Committee member Neville Clarke ran the youth team back then. "The team was extremely successful," remembers Bert, now turned 60. "We won everything as Neville got all the best local players. Some lovely people that come to mind that helped me in those days were Gordon 'Chippy' Hill, Geoff Heath and Arthur Chalkley."

At 17, Bert made his first team debut for Nantwich - a home game against Droylsden in the Manchester League in March 1966. Nantwich won 3-0 - and Hulse scored of course.

"From memory, I played for Nantwich as a teenager for 3-4 years and enjoyed every minute of it," adds Bert. "One of the managers during my time there was Alan Ball snr, the father of the late great Alan Ball - a World Cup winner with England. He had a lot of knowledge to pass on to anyone eager to learn. His first team in those days only had one professional - 'Sach' Groves. The rest were on expenses - 10 shillings for me."

Hulse's goalscoring prowess soon led to international recognition and the Nantwich starlet made his debut for England against Scotland in the Home International Youth tournament. Scotland won 1-0 but a few weeks later Hulse netted England's opener in a 3-0 win over Northern Ireland.

"I played 4 times for England Youth and scored 3 goals," recalls Bert who now resides in Cricklade, Wiltshire. "For the games in Dublin and Aberdeen, I roomed with our centre-half Larry Lloyd, then with Bristol Rovers. Larry, of course, went on to become a full international and twice won the European Cup with Nottingham Forest."

It's hardly surprising that Bert was snapped up by a bigger club and on 1st April 1967, he signed for Stoke City. "I played twice for Stoke's first team - against Sheffield United at home and away to Coventry the following season where I got kicked all over the park by Maurice Setters - a former team mate."

After a couple of years playing for Telford United under Ron Flowers (the former Wolves legend) an ankle injury ended his football career, but Bert continued to play cricket and enjoyed a few seasons with Nantwich under Maurice Mogg's captaincy.

ROBERT HULSE

Birthplace Crewe
Birthdate 5 November 1948
Nantwich Debut
v Droylsden, 26/3/66
Nantwich Goals
1965/66...1 (League)
1966/67...20 (9 Lge, 11 Cup)
England Youth Internationals
v Scotland (at Aberdeen) 4/2/67, lost 1-0
v Northern Ireland (at Stockport), 25/2/67, won 3-0
v Wales (at Cwmbran), 18/3/67, drew 3-3
v Republic of Ireland (at Dublin), 7/2/68, drew 0-0

BERT HULSE
Nantwich's 'Boy Wonder'

GETTING SHIRTY Bert's England shirt from his debut against Scotland & swapped shirts from other internationals, together with his England cap from the Home Internationals.

15-0 v Ashton United Reserves (home) 1966/67 Manchester League Division One, 25 Feb 1967
(Ashton Utd Reserves withdraw from the Manchester League during the season so the result was officially deleted from records)

15-1 v Audlem Town (home) 1946/47 Crewe Amateur Combination, 8 Mar 1947

14-1 v Rolls Royce (away) 1946/47 Crewe Amateur Combination, 12 Oct 1946

13-0 v Meadow Bank Swifts (home) 1895/96 Crewe & District Junior League, 11 Apr 1896

12-0 v Wrexham (home) 1907/08 The Combination, 8 Feb 1908

12-0 v Sandbach St Mary's Res (home) 1896/97 Crewe & District Junior Lge, 12 Sep 1896

12-1 v Nantwich GSOB 1958/59 Crewe & District FA Cup

12-1 v Newton-le-Willows (home) 1901/02 The Combination, 26 Dec 1901

12-3 v Hightak United (home) 1965/66 Gilgryst Cup 2nd Rd replay, 27 Nov 1965

11-0 v Audlem (away) 1946/47 Crewe Amateur Combination, 24 Mar 1947

11-1 v Moulton (home) 1964/65 Mid-Cheshire League

11-5 v Crewe Corinthians 1946/47 Commander Ethelston Cup Semi-Final (at Whitchurch) after extra time

10-0 v Skelmersdale United (home) 1994/95 NW Counties League Div 1, 11 Feb 1995

10-0 v Wrenbury Reserves (home) 1960/61 Crewe & District FA Cup 3rd Rd

10-0 v Coppenhall WMC (home) 1946/47 Crewe Amateur Combination, 3 May 1947

10-0 v Audlem (away) 1895/96 Crewe & District Junior League, 21 Sept 1895

10-1 v Buglawton Wolves (home) 1962/63 Crewe & District FA Cup

10-1 v Rolls Royce (home) 1947/48 Crewe & District Amateur League, 6 Sept 1947

9-0 v Bacup Borough (home) 1994/95 NW Counties League Div 1, 22 April 1995

9-0 v Radcliffe Borough Res (away) 1967/68 Manchester League

9-0 v Mossley Athletic (home) 1964/65 Mid-Cheshire League

9-0 v Basford Hall (away) 1946/47 Crewe Amateur Combination, 28 Dec 1946

9-0 v Middlewich (home) 1904/05 The Combination, 24 Apr 1905

9-1 v Goostrey (home) 1955/56 Cheshire Amateur Cup 1st Rd

9-1 v Altrincham Res (home) 1951/52 Mid-Cheshire League

9-1 v LMS Sports (away) 1947/48 Crewe & District Amateur League, 20 Dec 1947

9-1 v Chester (home) 1920/21 Cheshire County League, 19 Mar 1921

9-1 v Chester (home) 1902/03 The Combination, 14 Mar 1903

BIGGEST WINS

Nantwich first team games only

The following Saturday, the Dabbers hosted Ashton United Reserves in a Manchester League. At the time, Ashton's second string were struggling in the competitive First Division of the Manchester League and, as it turned out, they were unable to complete the season. It has to be said that Nantwich did little to help Ashton's cause on that Saturday afternoon in late February. The Dabbers totally outclassed the visitors and, by half time, the shell shocked Tamesiders were 8-0 down! And, there was no respite in the second half. By the time the referee brought proceedings to a close, Nantwich had recorded a 15-0 victory - a result that remains the club's biggest victory in its 125 year history. The scorers that memorable afternoon at London Road were: Max Brown (4), Jimmy Nichol (3), Cliff Slater (3), Alan Groves (2), Colin Corbishley, John Haughton and Martin Wells.

Perhaps the score would have been even bigger if scoring sensation Bert Hulse had been in the team that afternoon. However, Nantwich's young starlet, was on duty for England playing against Northern Ireland in a Youth International. In all, the local lad starred three times for England whilst a Nantwich player - a remarkable achievement.

Nantwich finished runners-up to New Mills at the end of the season and, the following campaign (1967/68) secured third place, with former Manchester City player Fred Kenny now at the helm. There was again a run to the quarter finals of the Cheshire Senior Cup. The drawing power the competition then enjoyed was again apparent. Over 1400 filled the London Road ground to watch a thrilling 3-3 draw against Witton Albion in the First Round. The Dabbers held the Cheshire League side to a goalless draw in the replay and a massive crowd of 4219 turned up to watch Mick Burrows net the only goal in the second replay, staged at Gresty Road, to send Nantwich through.

**MICK BURROWS
1966/67**

DABBERS SHOWED NO MERCY

THE Dabbers, dismissed from the Senior Cup last week, hit Ashton United with a tidal wave of goals when they resumed their Manchester League programme on Saturday. By half-time it was 7-0, and at the end of 90 minutes poor Ashton, in enough trouble down at the foot of the table, had taken a 15-0 beating.

Ashton began to get the drift of things as early as the second minute when a barrage on their goal ended like this: a Houghton shot rebounded from bar to Slater; his shot rebounded from bar to Brown; Brown nets.

In the eighth minute Slater made it 2-0 with an unstoppable shot. Brown headed the third in the 20th minute, and five minutes later completed his hat-trick.

Nantwich were now really getting their teeth into the match, and the next goal came from Groves who netted from the penalty spot after a header from Brown had been fisted out. No. 6 came in the 37th minute, when Slater hit the post and Brown slipped the rebound home; and No. 7 came a minute later when Groves smacked in a 20-yarder.

Already in more trouble than they knew how to handle, Ashton lost their goalkeeper early in the second half, and Samways, the substitute, took over.

He soon got into the back-bending act! Corbishley cruised up from centre-half to score the eighth, and further goals came from Nichol (3), Slater (2), Wells and Houghton.

Just to get the record straight, a complete recount of the goals shows these as the Nantwich marksmen: Brown (4), Slater (3), Nichol (3), Groves (2), Corbishley, Wells, Houghton (one each).

Team: Ward; Bayley, Kettle; Groves, Corbishley, Houghton; Wells, Nichol, Brown, Slater and Urmson.

This week the team, now well in the hunt for the Manchester League title, are away to Wigan Reserves.

There was no goal spree at Winnington, where Nantwich's Mid-Cheshire League side managed only a 1—1 draw. Nantwich had rather more of the game, and at half-time they were leading through a goal from Walkden.

Early in the second half, Marlow, Nantwich's new right-winger, hit the post, but that was the limit of the team's success. Winnington drew level when Tucker, the Nantwich 'keeper, dived to a shot but was unable to hold it. Nantwich pressed hard, but they lacked a marksman.

Team: Tucker; Morris, Capper; Lloyd, Pickford, Mehlmann; Marlow, Ravenscroft, Walkden, Jackson, Burrows.

This week the team are at home to Kidsgrove, kick-off 3.15 p.m.

☆ ☆ ☆

Bert Hulse, Nantwich's centre-forward, got his name on the scoresheet when he led England's youth international attack against Ireland at Stockport on Saturday. England won 3—0 and Bert notched the first goal.

☆ ☆ ☆

Salvador fought hard to beat Emberton Wanderers on Sunday

**EDDIE BROWN ...
led the scoring riot**

Barony Hospital 4, Lamb 4; Boot and Shoe 4, Vine (Nantwich) 4; Swan With Two Necks 3, Elelephant 5; B.B.B. 5, Willaston B.L. 3; Vine (Shavington) 5, Talbot 3, Three Pigeons 2, Red Lion 6.

Top scorers: J. Joyce (Talbot) 150; J. McDonald (Badger) 140; D. Young (Boot and Shoe) 137; R. Jones, (Vine, Nantwich) 134; E. Heath (Vine, Nantwich) 124; D. Wilkinson (Willaston B.L.) 122; F. Bickerton (Talbot) 120.

☆ ☆ ☆

Star A are making the Vine (Shavington) fight every inch of the way to retain their title in the Friday Darts League. Star won again last week and still lead Vine by two points.

Results: Millfields 1, Vine (Shavington) 7; Star B 4, Oddfellows 4; Nag's Head 2, Star A 6; Lord Combermere 2, Talbot 6; Tollemache 3, Game Cock 5; Red Lion (Barony) 3, Boot and Shoe 5; Railway 3, Red Lion A 5; Red Lion B 5, Shakespeare 3.

Top scorers: B. Taylor (Oddfellows) and G. France (Star A) 140; J. Lockett (Red Lion A) 139; F. Tudor (Star B) 117.

☆ ☆ ☆

NANTWICH, one of only two Cheshire clubs in the North Staffs and South Cheshire Cricket League, could end its long association with Staffordshire cricket, if a new Cheshire County proposal is accepted.

It is planned to form a Cheshire Cricket League—probably by about 1970—and Cheshire teams now competing in the N.S. and S.C. League, Manchester Association, Liverpool Competition and the Lancashire and Cheshire League, will be invited to join.

Speaking at a recent cricket dinner, Freddie Millett, captain of Cheshire, said he believed the County plan could be put into operation by 1970. He said: "We want to offer a service to Cheshire cricket, and the sooner we can all get together to play one another in one big all-embracing competition the better for the standard of the game". He added that most of the clubs who had already been notified of the proposal, seemed to welcome it.

Whether Nantwich would wish

**NANTWICH 15 ASHTON UNITED RESERVES 0
Manchester League, 25 February 1967**
Match report from the Nantwich Chronicle of 2nd March 1967, describing the club's biggest ever victory.

77

THE 40s, 50s & 60s

The disappointment of losing 2-0 at home to New Brighton in the Quarter-Finals was tempered by reaching the Gilgryst Cup Final. However, there was to be further disappointment as Eastwood Hanley cruised to a 5-1 two-legged victory. More importantly, the door to the Cheshire League was now pushed ajar as the formation of the new Northern Premier League created a number of vacancies in the county league.

SUPPORTING CREW
Secretary Jack Lindop (third from left) and Chairman Eddie Lockyer (fourth from left) supporting the team at Congleton in the 1960s. On the far left is milkman Jack Ellis, who played goalkeeper for the club and whose ashes were scattered on the old Jackson Avenue pitch.

Back in the fold

So (in the words of Baddiel and Skinner), the football folk of Nantwich had "never stopped believing" and, after "thirty years of hurt", the club was elected back to the golden land of the Cheshire County League in the summer of 1968.

The new era started with Buxton as visitors on 10th August 1968. The peculiarities of the fixture list saw the return fixture the following Wednesday with an early evening kick-off. Floodlights, of course, were yet to come into general use by non-league sides.

The home game saw Nantwich go down 3-0 and Buxton secured an early season double, winning the return game 3-1, Ray King netting Nantwich's first goal on the club's return to the Cheshire League. The following week, a goal by Cliff Hodgkinson gave Nantwich a 1-0 win over Witton Albion as the Dabbers chalked up their first league victory. Hodgkinson (who later had a short spell as Manager in 1986) finished the season as leading scorer with 26 goals,

**RAY KING
1968/69**
Scorer of Nantwich's first goal on the return to the Cheshire League

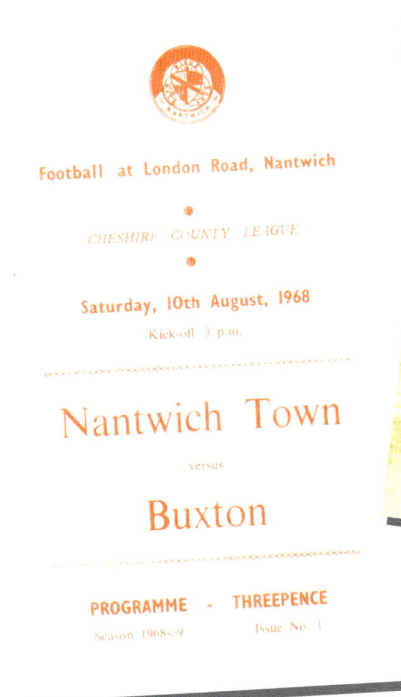

**NANTWICH v BUXTON - 1968/69
Official Programmes**
The first home and first away games after returning to the Cheshire League.

BIG JACK

Jack (left), in 1990, receiving from Neville Clarke an award in recognition of his long service to the club

Anyone who had anything to do with the football club in the 60s, 70s or 80s knew 'Big Jack' - as simple as that. Jack Lindop was a terrific servant of the club, becoming Secretary in 1959 and serving for over three decades until he sadly suffered a severe stroke in 1991. For more than ten years, he also combined secretarial duties with the role of Chairman!

A foreman fitter at Crewe Works, Jack was awarded the Secretary of the Year prize for the Cheshire County League in 1974. Talking at the time he commented, "My only wish is that we could attract more local players to the team." Jack, himself, was certainly never afraid of getting his hands dirty in the cause of the local club. "I used to mark out the pitch on a Saturday morning, dash home for lunch and get back to the ground in time for the afternoon match. Many a time I used to have only a ten minute break for lunch," he recalled back then.

The sight of Jack on his old pushbike, gently pedalling up Jackson Avenue to the old ground, will be remembered by many. Life member Neville Clarke has fond memories of the big man. "Like many of us back in those days, we were employed in Crewe Works. The talk there would always be about football. From time to time, though, there were matters relating to the football club that couldn't wait until the next Committee Meeting. I was Assistant Secretary so Jack would call me into the Engine Room and we'd have an impromptu meeting there on some pressing matter!"

At the time, the club relied heavily on a weekly fundraising Tote to help pay its way. "We had an old 'Gestetner' machine in the small Secretary's Office at Jackson Avenue," recalls Neville. "You attached a typed stencil sheet to the barrel and when you turned the handle rapidly, it would pull paper through and print off what was on the stencil. Well, one morning I was in the canteen and I could hear all sorts of swearing and foul language shouting out from the office. It was Big Jack. He hadn't put the bung in the ink tank - and when he'd whipped the stencil drum round, ink had splattered everywhere – all over the office walls and on his tie and suit!"

Before becoming Nantwich Secretary, Jack had spent nine years as a referee and took charge of many local finals. He also acted as Master of Ceremonies for the LMR Boxing Club in Crewe. But football was always Jack's first sport and it was cruel that the stroke should later prevent him continuing his active participation in it. Another blow came when his beloved wife Molly passed away in 1997 and subsequently Jack moved out of his home in Park View into Rosedale Manor Care Home in Crewe.

Jack's contribution to Nantwich Town Football Club can never be under estimated. Working with Chairman Eddie Lockyer, Treasurer Gordon McDonald and an enthusiastic Committee, he was instrumental in turning the club from a mid-table Mid-Cheshire League side with hefty debts into a top Cheshire County League outfit. Like many, his proudest memory was of the club winning the old Cheshire League title back in 1981. He sadly passed away in October 2008 at the age of 84.

BACK IN THE FOLD

followed on 16 goals by King, the ex-Tranmere forward.

Former Grimsby Town coach Len Traynor had taken over as Manager at the beginning of the campaign. Assisted by Keith Randles and with David Morgans as captain, he was able to steer the club to a satisfactory 12th position in the league by the end of the season.

Club finances were again coming into the spotlight and it had cost £1400 more to run the team in the Cheshire League than in the previous season. As preparations were made for a second season in the Cheshire League, Dr Kenneth Kay accepted the role of club President, which had previously been filled by Peter Wilson, and Gordon McDonald was appointed Treasurer in succession to Russell Crank who himself had taken over from Robert Lomas. Manager of the Trustee Savings Bank in Nantwich, Gordon's financial acumen ensured the club continued in operation over the next few decades. Gordon's son, Ian remembers his father giving Chairman Eddie Lockyer a lift to matches. "With being blind, Eddie used to have a commentary recorded every week," recalls Ian. "My Dad used to dread Eddie's commentator not turning up in case he had to commentate the whole match whilst Eddie recorded it and listened again on Saturday evening. Dad didn't fancy himself as a David Coleman!"

The summer of 1969 and the whole of the world was glued to their small black and white TV sets. "One small step for man, one giant step for mankind," crackled Neil Armstrong as he became the first man on the moon. Meanwhile, back at base, ex-Leeds United player Terry Casey was now in command. Although the Dabbers dropped to 16th in the league, they fought through to the semi-finals of the Cheshire Senior Cup for the first time in over 30 years. Middlewich, Moulton, Barnton, Macclesfield and Runcorn were all despatched on the way to the semi against Hyde United at Macclesfield's Moss Rose ground. There was heartbreak for Nantwich, though, and despite two goals from John Sealey, the Dabbers went down 5-2.

LEN TRAYNOR
Manager 1968/69
He later went on to become Manager at Chorley, Netherfield, Southport and Droylsden

TERRY CASEY
Manager 1969/70

BACK IN THE FOLD

**HAROLD CLARKE
1970**

Pictured here with the newly completed grandstand in the background, Harold had joined the club Committee in 1947. His brother, Tom, had previously been club trainer and Harold went on to become groundsman. He served as groundsman for 12 years, stepping down at the age of 78 in October 1973. When he passed away in May 1974, the club purchased a bench in his memory which was placed at the bottom of Jackson Avenue. Harold's son, Neville, followed in his footsteps, having joined the Committee in 1959.

The early 70s saw Nantwich struggle to compete at Cheshire League level (finishing bottom in 1971/72) but the appointment of former Stafford Rangers Manager Colin Hutchinson in January 1973 was to lead to a revival of fortunes. It was to co-incide with the club formally adding the suffix 'Town' to its title. Although, the Dabbers had come to be known as 'Nantwich Town' for a number of years, it wasn't until late in 1973 that the change of name was officially registered with the Football Association.

The 1973/74 season had seen Nantwich reach the First Round Proper of the FA Trophy - a competition which had been introduced in 1969 for non-league's top dogs. Fortune had favoured the Dabbers who, after a Preliminary Round bye, were drawn at home in all three qualifying rounds. Winsford United and New Brighton were both defeated 2-1 whilst two goals from ex-Stafford Rangers and Doncaster Rovers front man Keith Mottershead secured a 2-0 win over Accrington Stanley in the final qualifying round. Sadly, Nantwich's luck ran out and, drawn away to local rivals Sandbach

BACK IN THE FOLD

Ramblers, the Dabbers sadly crashed out of the Trophy on the back of a 3-0 defeat.

In October Harold Clarke had stepped down after 12 years' service as groundsman and, sadly, he passed away the following May. Henry Palin took over groundsman's duties to be succeeded a few years later by Peter Temmen, who had joined the Committee in June 1971. Jack Lindop was named as Cheshire League Secretary of the Year and some serious stuff was brought up at the 1974 AGM. A supporter

Nantwich Town's league record season-by-season since 1973 can be viewed at the Football Club History Database.
Visit: www.fchd.info/NANTWICT.HTM

THE FOOTBALL ASSOCIATION
LIMITED
Patron: HER MAJESTY THE QUEEN
President: H.R.H. THE DUKE OF KENT
Chairman: SIR ANDREW STEPHEN, M.B., Ch.B.

Secretary: E. A. CROKER

Telegraphic Address: FOOTBALL ASSOCIATION, LONDON, W2 3LW

16 LANCASTER GATE, LONDON, W2 3LW

Our Ref: H/CDT   Your Ref:

10th December, 1973

J. Lindop, Esq.,
Nantwich F.C.,
13 Park View,
Nantwich, Cheshire

Dear Sir,

Change of Name

I am writing to inform you that the Council at its meeting held on 26th November, acceded to your request to change the name of your Club from Nantwich F.C. to Nantwich Town F.C.

Yours faithfully,

for Secretary

Registered Office: 16 Lancaster Gate, London, W2 3LW
Incorporated in London   Registration Number 77797

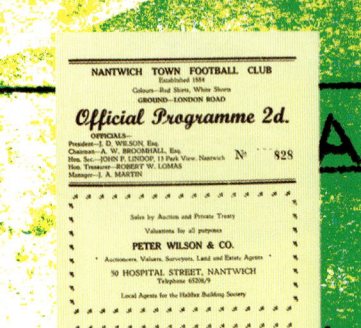

1961/62 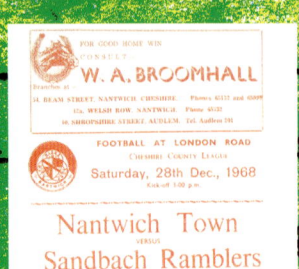    **1968/69** 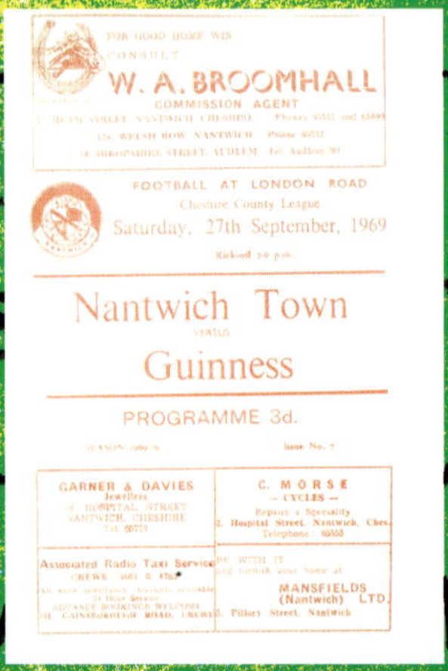   **1969/70**    **1970/71**

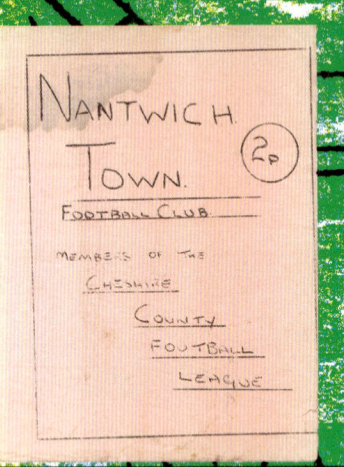

1971/72    **1972/73** 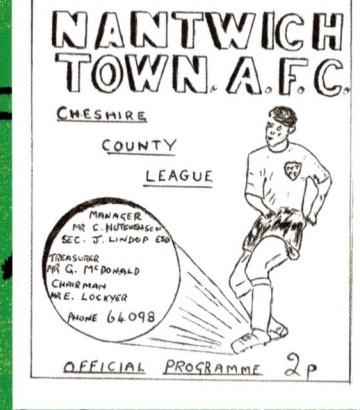   **1973/74 & 74/75**

PROGRAMMES
1960s & 1970s

Although most Cheshire League clubs produced programmes before the Second World War, it is not known that Nantwich did - the club's poor attendances just wouldn't have made it worthwhile! With the club reverting to less senior leagues after the War, it wasn't until the club returned to the Cheshire County League in 1968 that programmes became a regular feature at London Road - though there had been a brief flirtation with issuing in the latter half of the 1961/62 Mid-Cheshire League campaign.

After having them professionally printed in 1968/69 & 69/70, the club programme became a basic home-produced (but quaint) edition through the 70s when the good old-fashioned hand cranked Gestetner machine in the tiny old club office would churn out scarcely more than a handful of ink-smudged two penny offerings.

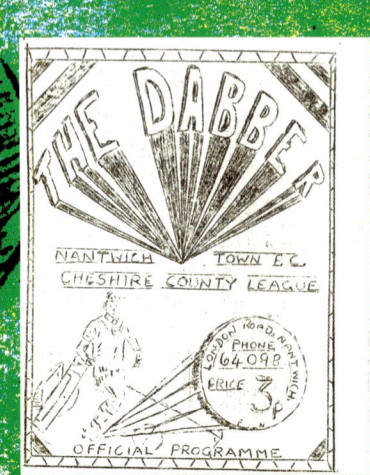

1976/77 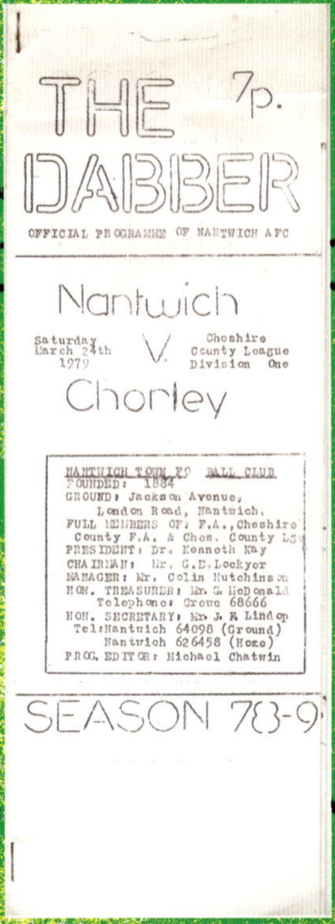   **1978/79**    **1979/80**

BACK IN THE FOLD

asked whether it would be possible to make the cups of tea a bit stronger. Gwen Knowles, who served the club so well for many years as canteen manageress, said this was the first complaint she'd had but that she would certainly look into the matter.

Hutchinson made George Machin his captain for the 1974/75 season but it was a player named Johnny Walker who was to grab the headlines. Walker struck 15 goals that season and when Hutchinson brought in Brian Griffin from Prestwich Heys during the 1975 close season, the pair formed a lethal partnership fit to terrorise the meanest of Cheshire League defences.

Their strike force helped the Dabbers finish a creditable 6th in the league in 1975/76 but the season is best remembered for a thrilling campaign in the Cheshire Senior Cup.

Although Walker missed out in the 2-0 home win over Barnton, he chipped in with a brace to knock out Altrincham 2-1 in the next round. Then, in the Semi-Final at Winsford, Walker's first half double eliminated further Northern Premier opposition when Macclesfield Town were defeated 2-1.

Walker's goals set up Nantwich for their seventh Cheshire Senior Cup Final and their first since that tense victory over ICI Alkali 43 years earlier. Nantwich's opponents at Gresty Road - the regular haunt for Senior Cup

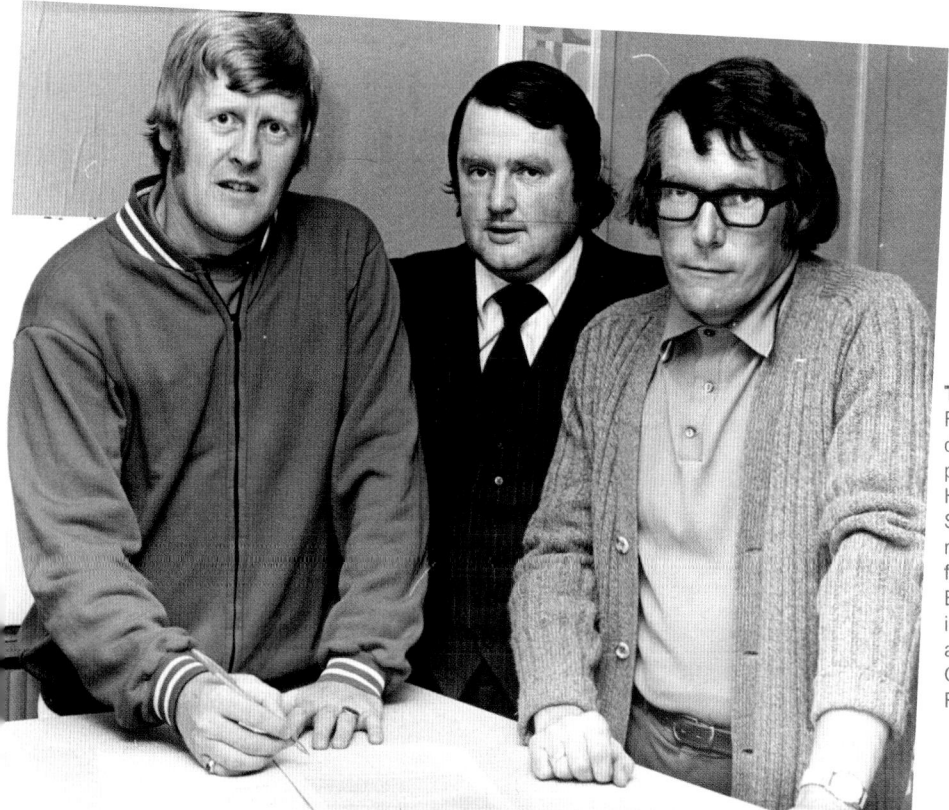

COLIN CHADWICK
Colin had helped Whitchurch Alport to the Mid-Cheshire League title and Shropshire Amateur Cup in 1969/70. He scored 55 goals for Whitchurch during the 1970/71 season, earning a step up to Cheshire League football with Nantwich for the 1971/72 campaign. He soon made a big impression at the higher level, and after netting 11 goals was snapped up midway through the season by Wigan Athletic - then in the Northern Premier League.

TONY ALLEN
Former Stoke City and England defender Tony Allen puts pen to paper watched by Manager Colin Hutchinson (centre) and Assistant Secretary Neville Clarke (right). Tony made over 400 League appearances for The Potters before moving on to Bury in October 1970. He had spells in South Africa with Cape Town City and Hellenic, returning to England in October 1973. He played for Stafford Rangers before joining Nantwich.

BACK IN THE FOLD

DAY TO REMEMBER FOR DABBERS

**NANTWICH TOWN 5
RUNCORN 4**

AFTER a pulsating, nerve-tingling Cheshire Senior Cup final at Gresty Road, Crewe, on Saturday, proud Nantwich Town finally overcame a Runcorn side, which it seemed just would not lie down and die.

But it took them 120 minutes to do it. At the end of 90 minutes' thrilling football, the teams were still at a 4-4 deadlock. Then, three minutes into the second period of extra time, Johnny Walker Nantwich's irrepressible goal machine, pounced again, and finally Runcorn were finished.

As Nantwich Skipper Bev. Wilson took the trophy from Mr. Billy Gray, Vice-president of Cheshire F.A., there were many among the Nantwich fans who could recall the last occasion they won it way back in 1933. For those old-time supporters, it was a day they will never forget.

Nantwich began with their nerves showing. They were over-anxious and did not seem to know what to do with the ball when they had it. After six minutes Andy Carr crashed the ball into his own net as he tried to clear a cross from the right, and Nantwich hearts sank. Surely Runcorn, Senior Cup experts, would cash in on such a gift.

But within a minute Nantwich were level. The ball swirled in from the left and Brian Griffin rose to nod it in.

Shortlived

Now Nantwich were in high glee, but it was shortlived. Less than a minute later they trailed again as Whitbread slotted the ball past Cutler from a suspiciously-looking offside position.

But if Nantwich were rather timid in the first half, they were transformed after the break. With 28 minutes to go Walker had a shot charged down and Andy Scott coolly flipped the loose ball home to make it 2-2. Eight minutes later Nantwich fans hit the roof as Walker hurtled down the left to steer the ball home with all his usual confidence.

Once again Runcorn hit back, this time through Finnigan from the penalty spot after Anthony had accidentally handled.

With five minutes left it was Nantwich's turn for a penalty. Scott was dragged down just inside the box and Walker's deadly left foot did the rest — Nantwich 4, Runcorn 3.

Still Runcorn would not accept defeat and Whitbread headed in the goal which once more pulled them level. So it went into extra time. The first period passed fairly peacefully after all that had gone before.

But in the final 15 minutes Nantwich at last battered Runcorn into submission. Jones, who had come on as sub for the exhausted Griffin, flicked the ball through the middle and Walker's deceptive pace swept him clear of the defence and once more the goal which followed was a formality.

Now there was no time for Runcorn to come back and as the whistle went Town manager Colin Hutchinson raced on to the pitch to congratulate a team which had done him and "Dabtown" proud.

Nantwich: Cutler; Patton, Fowles; Anthony, Wilson, Sherratt; Handley, Carr, Griffin, Walker, Scott. Sub.: Jones.
Runcorn: Rawlinson; Baker, Rutter; Bailey, Duff, King; Hipwell, Wilson, Whitbread, Finnigan, Howard. Sub.: Cocks.
Referee: Mr. G. Nolan, Hazel Grove. Attendance: 2,247.

Finals at the time - were high-flying Runcorn. In that pre-Conference era, the Linnets were acknowledged as one of the top semi-pro sides in England and were crowned champions of the Northern Premier League at the end of the campaign.

There was eager anticipation amongst the Nantwich faithful but no-one could have anticipated the drama to come. As the Chronicle match report shows, it was a see-saw game that was edge of the seat stuff. By the time referee Mr Nolan blew at the end of a pulsating 120 minutes, the Dabbers had triumphed 5-4 - thanks largely to a superb hat-trick from who else but Johnny Walker.

Nantwich's captain Bev Wilson stepped up to receive the trophy from Cheshire FA Vice-President Billy Gray who, appropriately enough, had previously been Secretary of Nantwich and a loyal servant of the club.

It was a great all-round team performance from the Nantwich lads. Cutler, like one of his successors Alan Ryder, was a capable keeper who had been on Stoke City's books. Eddie Patton and Les Anthony were ex-Stafford Rangers players who would team up again later in their careers with Joe Handley at Hednesford Town. Gary Fowles, a policeman, proved a loyal servant to Nantwich over the years and had previously been with Crewe Alex as a youngster. Alan Sherratt, David Jones and Andy Scott (who had been brought in for a

JUBILIATION
Nantwich captain Bev Wilson holds aloft the Cheshire Senior Cup

1976 Cheshire Senior Cup Final
Nantwich 5
Runcorn 4 after extra time
10th April 1976
at Gresty Road, Crewe   Attendance: 2247

1 ADRIAN CUTLER
2 EDDIE PATTON
3 GARY FOWLES
4 LES ANTHONY
5 BEV WILSON
6 ALAN SHERRATT
7 JOE HANDLEY
8 ANDY CARR
9 BRIAN GRIFFIN
10 JOHNNY WALKER
11 ANDY SCOTT
12 DAVID JONES

BACK IN THE FOLD

£100 fee the previous November) were all former Macclesfield Town players. Wilson had joined Nantwich from Northwich Victoria for a fee of £150 (+ £12 VAT !) and had gained considerable League experience in Stockport County's rearguard. The bearded Carr had begun footballing life at Port Vale where he made a single senior start in an FA Cup tie at Luton Town. He teamed up with the Dabbers from Northwich Victoria and commanded a £400 fee when he moved on to Leek Town in December 1977. He later re-joined Nantwich having had spells with Droylsden and Macclesfield Town.

NANTWICH TOWN - CHESHIRE SENIOR CUP WINNERS 1976
Back Row (left to right): Keith Randles (trainer), Brian Griffin, David Jones, Bob Walters (coach)
Middle Row: Joe Handley, Gary Fowles, Adrian Cutler, Peter Gowans, Alan Sherratt, Johnny Walker
Front Row: Andy Carr, Les Anthony, Bev Wilson, Colin Hutchinson (Manager), Eddie Patton, Andy Scott.

BACK IN THE FOLD

In 1976/77, Nantwich again finished in a healthy 6th spot in the league and made a valiant attempt to defend the Senior Cup. Having overcome Chester and Stockport County, the Dabbers bowed out 2-1 to Northwich Victoria in the semi-finals.

A £400 fee took Griffin to Witton Albion in March 1977 and in October, Walker moved on to Leek Town before teaming up again with his old strike partner at Witton. The devastating duo later switched to Macclesfield Town, then a powerful force in the Northern Premier League. In just four seasons at London Road (two of which were not full campaigns), Walker netted 95 goals for the club.

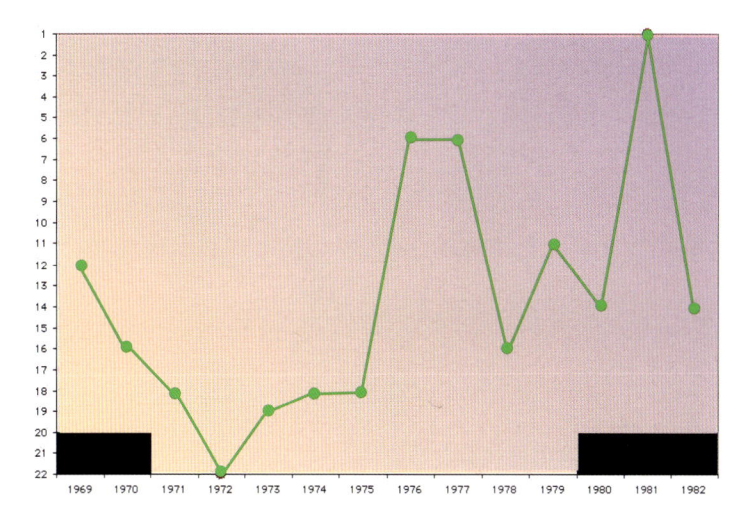

CHESHIRE LEAGUE PROGRESS
A chart plotting the The Dabbers' league positions during their second spell in the Cheshire County League from 1968 to 1982. (Only 20 clubs competed in 1968/69 & 69/70, 79/80-81/82)

PAUL MAYMAN
1977/78
With a promising career outside football, 'Mayo' turned his back on the professional ranks. The gifted 19 year old signed for Nantwich in the summer of 1977 having made 42 League appearances for Crewe Alexandra and was soon made club captain. The talented midfielder later moved on to Northwich Victoria where he became a key figure as the Vics became founder members of the Alliance Premier League (later known as The Conference) in 1979. He was twice capped for the England Semi-Professional XI.

My own first memories of the club were when 'Hutch' was still in charge. In those days, not all Cheshire League clubs issued a match day programme. Having produced a distinctly home grown effort in the early 70s, Nantwich had stopped issuing programmes so my offer to edit and print one was welcomed by the Committee. In the days before photocopiers and computers, I would bash out each page on a stencil sheet with an old Smith Corona typewriter. I'd then run them off on an inky Gestetner machine in the office at my father's bakery. I was disappointed with the trial run - a home game against Chorley at the tail end of the 1978/79 season. There wasn't the right size paper to hand, so outsize folded card had to suffice. On match day, I took them to the ground and apologetically showed them to Neville Clarke who was then Assistant Secretary. Neville was having none of it. "That's champion!" he enthused about my cobbled together affair.

The old ground in those days was a picture to behold, particularly at the start of the season. The stand and large old trees provided a fine backdrop along the Crewe Road side of the pitch and, opposite, a

BACK IN THE FOLD

row of poplars swaying gently in the breeze framed the picture. The ground oozed pride and Jack Lindop and his merry band of helpers always had it in pristine condition. Behind the goal at the Jackson Avenue end, two large wooden pavilions housed all the necessaries (there was no Social Club in those days). Two single turnstiles flanked the main iron gate which clattered open to let in the handful of cars which could park on the ground. Through the turnstiles, the pavilion on the right housed the home and away dressing rooms (which were connected by a shared bath!) and a separate changing room for the match officials - not big enough for swinging the proverbial cat.

**BOB WALTERS
1979/80**
The Nantwich Manager (right) surveys a veritable forest of facial hair in his dressing room.

The wooden pavilion on the left was a mirror image; the glorified cupboard serving as the 'Secretary's Office' whilst the main part housed a cavernous canteen - the preserve of Gwen Knowles and later Kay Livingstone and Olga Pye. Here, Neville Clarke and Albert Pye would host midweek bingo sessions to raise much needed funds for the club. On matchdays, though, this was the haven to grab a hot cuppa to ward off the elements - and if that didn't scald your mouth, you could be sure a cheese & onion pasty would. "The fillings were like molten lava," recalls supporter Gary Cliffe who had started following the club as a boy and whose sister, Gaynor, later married the very Steve Davis who went on to become the most successful manager in the club's history.

LEADING SCORERS
Cheshire League Days

69/70
John Sealey   20 goals

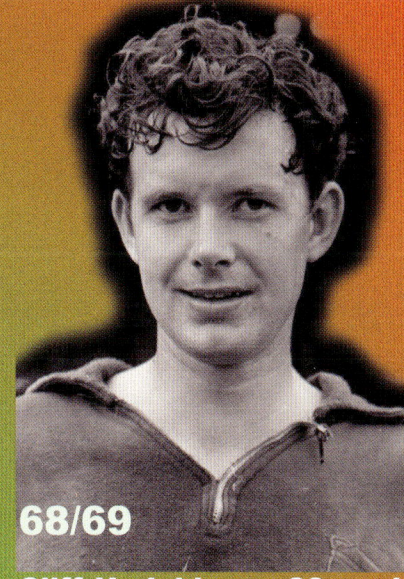

68/69
Cliff Hodgkinson 26 goals

73/74
Max Brown   16 goals

78/79
Paul Reid   18 goals

70/71
Derek Smith   14 goals

79/80 & 80/81
Kevin Westwood
79/80 **15 goals** & 80/81 **29 goals**

BACK IN THE FOLD

DAVE JENNINGS
1980/81
A speedy left winger signed from Eastwood Hanley in the 1980 close season.

Like many, Gary also remembers the pitch invasion that followed the title-clinching game against Hyde United in April 1981. It's as though that game - and the pitch invasion that followed - is indelibly marked on the psyche of Dabber fans of the time.

Perhaps it's hardly surprising. 1976 Cheshire Senior Cup aside, Nantwich fans were starved of success. The club had finished 14th in the 1979/80 season under Bob Walters, the former Stafford Rangers centre-half who stepped up after Colin Hutchinson had taken up the reins at Droylsden. Jimmy Wallace had been installed as Manager at the start of the 1980/81 campaign but there was nothing to suggest that, come May, Nantwich would scoop the Cheshire League prize that had always been well beyond their grasp.

A former League footballer with Stoke City and Doncaster Rovers, Jimmy had played non-league for Northwich Victoria and Stafford Rangers. The previous season, he had guided Eastwood Hanley to 6th place in the Second Division of the Cheshire League. He brought with him to Nantwich the cream of that Eastwood side - Nigel Brattle, Denis Roden, Richie Bloor, Mick Cartwright, John Harrison and Dave Jennings - and they were to prove to be the backbone of the Dabbers' championship winning side.

Rise and fall

Back in 1980, Margaret Thatcher was still settling in at Downing Street as Britain's first female Prime Minister. The synthesised sound of Gary Numan was ushering in an era of new wave and Jimmy Wallace's new-look Nantwich side were quickly making music of their own.

With former Winsford United centre half Ted Neale as captain, the Dabbers were soon heading up the Cheshire League charts - losing just once in their opening 15 league games. The squad was further strengthened with the addition of John Kelley from Port Vale and two signings from Droylsden - former Cheshire Senior Cup winner Andy Carr and Tony Loska who had bundles of League experience with Port Vale and Chester. Sadly, though, there was a blip in form over Christmas and with Hyde United's consistently good results, it seemed as though the title would head to Tameside. Paul Reid, the Dabbers' leading marksman, was snapped up by Alliance Premier neighbours Northwich Victoria in January leaving Wallace's challengers potentially short of firepower.

There was further setback in February when a large poplar tree blew over in strong winds at the Jackson Avenue ground, smashing through the roof of the cover on the popular side.

However, with goalkeeper Alan Ryder in inspirational form, four clean sheets in February and early March got the challenge back on track. Former Crewe Alex striker Ted White was drafted in to lead the line as Nantwich sought to mount a late push. Having been top of the table since August, Hyde started to drop points and it

JIM WALLACE
Manager 1980/81

STORM DAMAGE
February 1981

RISE AND FALL

coincided with the Dabbers hitting a purple patch of late season form. A sequence of six back-to-back wins in the space of 17 days eroded what had seemed the Tigers' insurmountable lead. Ashton United were beaten 5-1, Kevin Westwood grabbed four goals in a comprehensive 7-1 win at St Helens Town whilst Burscough (2-0), Bootle (5-0), Darwen (4-0) and Stalybridge Celtic (2-0) were all put to the sword as the Dabbers went on the rampage scoring 26 goals and conceeding just one in that six game sequence.

Fate conspired that the two clubs should meet in a title decider at Nantwich on 2nd May. A win for either side would give them the Cheshire League crown. A draw and Nantwich would need to beat Leek Town at home in their remaining fixture.

Alan Jervis, the long serving Dabbers correspondent, captured the momentous 2-1 victory in his Nantwich Chronicle report.

It was a terrific achievement for the club to top the Cheshire League. Never before had the Dabbers come close to challenging for the title - and neither would they again - not even in the North West Counties League which was formed in 1982 by the Cheshire League's amalgamation with the Lancashire Combination.

Sadly, the championship-winning team soon broke up. A month after the season's end, 29 goal top scorer Kevin Westwood went to Stafford Rangers for a fee of £1443. Without 'Westy's' goals, the Champions made a stuttering start to the 1981/82 campaign - winning just two of the opening 8 league fixtures. In October, championship chief Jimmy Wallace took over the reins at neighbouring Leek Town and soon after Ted White moved on to Whitchurch Alport.

Financial pressures were also starting to bite. The surge to win the title hadn't brought a huge response at the turnstile (the average attendance in 1980/81 was only 312) so the club had finished the season £1300 overdrawn. By November, the club was £1900 in the red and when John Archer was appointed as the new Manager in January 1982, he had to cut his cloth accordingly with any hopes of retaining the title long since gone.

History makers!

NANTWICH TOWN 2, HYDE UNITED 1

THE scoreline tells it all. Nantwich Town, after a magnificent run-in to the season, are champions of the Cheshire League for the first time in their history (WRITES ALAN JERVIS).

But after 89 minutes of this pulsating match, it looked as if Hyde, had won the two-horse race for the title. This was their last match of the season, and a victory would have given them the championship. They were in the lead through a 79th minute goal from Bloor, and it looked as if Nantwich's run of six successive wins was going to count for nothing.

Then in an incredible 60 seconds, Nantwich turned defeat into victory to send a large proportion of the 1,078 fans wild with delight.

First Ted White smashed in a screaming 15 yard drive which Hyde goalkeeper D'Arcy barely saw. And then while Hyde were still rocking from their unexpected setback, Kevin Westwood raced through to plant in the winner, and all the pent-up suspense of the crowd exploded as the pitch was invaded.

There was scarcely time to re-start the game before the final whistle went, and the Dabbers, founded way back in 1884, had pulled off their greatest success.

Within seconds of the end of the game, players and fans celebrated in a shower of champagne outside the dressing rooms.

Nantwich will receive the Cheshire League trophy on May 14 when they take on Hyde again at London Road in the traditional match between the champions and runners-up.

Tomorrow, Thursday, the team play Winsford at London Road in the semi-final of the Cheshire League Cup, and they will be going all-out to reach the final, and complete a Cup and League double.

Nantwich's long serving secretary, Jack Lindop, was naturally delighted when he spoke to "The Chronicle" after the match. He said: "All credit to the players and manager Jim Wallace, who has done a remarkable job. This is the greatest day in our history."

READ ALL ABOUT IT

For many years, Chronicle reporter **Alan Jervis** was the voice of Nantwich Football Club. Here, he recalls some of his memories of reporting on The Dabbers.

The date April 10 1976:

The match Nantwich v Runcorn in the Cheshire Senior Cup Final at Gresty Road:

The result 5-4 to Nantwich after extra time.

It was a game I will never forget, as the Dabbers came from behind to outlast their more fancied opponents - thanks to a hat-trick from Johnny Walker, perhaps the best striker I have seen in nearly 60 years watching Nantwich - and a goal apiece from Andy Scott and Brian Griffin.

I don't think I have ever seen a more exciting game at any level - well maybe the 1966 World Cup Final!

ANDY SCOTT

My earliest memories of watching Nantwich - not Nantwich Town in those days - were in the very early 1950s.

In those days teams were allowed two professionals - ours were centre-half Ernie Tagg, later to become Crewe Alex manager, and Jimmy Cooke, a skillful inside-forward.

Incidentally, the ground was always referred to back then as London Road - the Jackson Avenue tag came much later.

Down the years there have been many 'characters' associated with the Dabbers. Fans will have their own thoughts, but players who stick out in my mind include centre-forward Jack Young who, in the days before they became a protected species, was likely to put the goalkeeper (and maybe the centre-half as well) into the back of the net along with the ball if they happened to be in his path as he rose for a header.

And what about Herbie Sandland, a centre-half who seemed to be able to head a ball - remember those big soggy 'casies' - as far as most people could kick it.

A brilliant all-round local sportsman, Herbie once hit a century and took all 10 wickets in the same match in the Nantwich Cricket Knock-out, which by the way was played on the Jackson Avenue football ground back then.

There were many more: Geoff Heath, a right-winger who seemed to have been playing forever; the thunderous shooting Denis Nicholls, the powerhouse midfielder Peter Moulton; many years later Johnny Walker who I have already mentioned; his strike partner Brian Griffin; and in the days when Alan Ball senior was manager, the artistic yet powerful inside-forward Jimmy Fletcher.

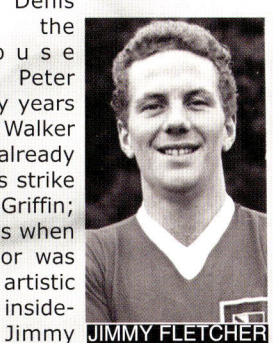

JIMMY FLETCHER

I recall Mr Ball seemed to like having players called Taylor in his teams - sometimes as many as five the same day. You can draw your own conclusions from that!

I wonder how many regular followers can recall the 1985-86 season, when the team had almost as many managers as players!

Dave Cooke began the season in charge, with Dave Nixon his assistant.

Cooke lasted only a few weeks before he quit to be replaced by Nixon and Ian Cooke.

Exit Nixon to be replaced by Ian Cooke and Ernie Blunstone. And it didn't end there. The season ended with Cliff Hodgkinson in charge. Phew!

In the days before things became quite as professional as they are now, it was not unknown for match day to arrive without a full quota of officials.

One day enter Reg 'Dickie' Drew, a diehard Dabbers supporter, who offered to help out by running the line. His offer was taken up but after a short time the referee suggested he had better stand down as Nantwich seemed to be benefitting rather too much from his flag waving!

Talking of linesman, as they still were then, I can recall standing with a group of supporters maybe a dozen or so years ago, and having a little friendly banter with one of them as he ran the touchline on the side of the 'new' stand.

He seemed, if not exactly enjoying it, to be taking it in good heart.

Just then he flagged for offside, when there was clearly a defender standing almost on the goalkeeper's toes. His clanger was pointed out to him in no uncertain terms.

To his credit, the next time he ran past us, he turned, winked, and said: `I never noticed him!'

They are just a few random memories from childhood fan, to reporter, to pensioner.

Maybe they should not be concluded without mentioning Jack Lindop, the long serving Secretary in the London Road days, Eddie Lockyer, a marvellous blind man who was Chairman for many years during the same period, and their hard working Committee. Now both deceased I am sure they would both be thrilled with where the Dabbers are today.

RISE AND FALL

CHESHIRE LEAGUE CHAMPIONS 1980/81

Players pictured are:
Standing (left to right): Ritchie Bloor, Alan Ryder, Kevin Roche, John Harrison, Kevin Westwood, Ted Neale (with trophy), Kevin Everett, Gary Fowles, Jim Wallace (Manager), Tony Loska. Kneeling: Dave Jennings, Ted White, Mick Cartwright.

By the end of the season, the Dabbers had slumped to 14th. Centre half Kevin Roche was offered the position of player-manager at Eastwood Hanley and when he left, Richie Bloor, Mick Cartwright, Kevin Everett and Denis Roden followed. With Alan Ryder and Dave Jennings joining Congleton Town there was little of the championship winning side left when Nantwich kicked off the 1982/83 season in the new North West Counties League.

NANTWICH TOWN 0, RHYL 4
14 August 1982
Nantwich's teamsheet for the club's first game in the North West Counties League.

click4more

All final league tables for the North West Counties League can be viewed on-line.
Visit:
www.rsssf.com/tablese/engnwcleaghist.html

96

RISE AND FALL

The rot had now started to set in. Former Crewe Alex and Nantwich midfielder Peter Gowans replaced John Archer in the hot seat but the Dabbers lost their first 12 games in the new league. A merry-go-round of Managers was now spinning with former Congleton Town boss Roy Campbell in charge for the second half of a disastrous season which saw Nantwich finish bottom - and relegated to the Second Division of the NWCL.

Life was little less comfortable at this lower level. Assistant Mick Pickup had stepped up after Campbell left to become Assistant Manager at Macclesfield Town during the 1983 close season. Only three wins were chalked up in the opening 14 league matches and when the roundabout stopped again, Pickup hopped off and former Liverpool winger and England international Alan A'Court jumped on. The ex-Stoke City coach was unable to bring any respite and the club ended the season propping up the Second Division of the NWCL.

Dave Cooke and Ernie Blunstone took over as joint-managers for the 84/85 season as Nantwich finished 11th. 'Cookie' was given sole charge at the start of the following campaign but gave way to Dave

NANTWICH TOWN 2
WARRINGTON TOWN 3
13 August 1983
Official Programme from the Dabbers' first game in the Second Division of the North West Counties League.

CENTENARY CELEBRATION
June 1984
Club President Dr Kenneth Kay (left) and Treasurer Gordon McDonald make a presentation to Jack Lindop (right) to mark his 25th anniversary as club Secretary.

RISE AND FALL

NANTWICH TOWN - 1985/86
Back Row (left to right): Billy Heath, Kevin Westwood, Pete Blundell, Neil Ridgway, Derek Fortune, Austin Salmon, Steve Wright, Ian Wheaton, Dave Nixon (Assistant Manager).
Front Row: Peter Kettle (mascot), Kevin Hinett, Dave Cooke (Player-Manager), Mark Fallon, Steve Piggott, Mark Flanaghan.

Nixon in December 1985. Just a month later a new managerial team was installed as Ian Cooke and Ernie Blunstone were put in joint control. By March 1986, former player Cliff Hodgkinson was named as another new boss but another humiliating season ended with Nantwich finishing bottom and relegated to the North West Counties League Third Division.

Glyn Morris dared to take over the Nantwich hot seat in August 1986 with the Dabbers rubbing shoulders with the likes of Daisy Hill, Maghull and Whitworth Valley. It looked as though things were at last starting to improve with Morris guiding his charges to joint top. The January Manager of the Month award, though, carried its customary curse. A run of 12 games without victory saw the club drop like a lead weight. By the end of that 1986/87 season, Nantwich had finished 11th out of 13 clubs in the NWCL Third Division. It was, perhaps, the club's lowest ebb.

But, from the bottom, the only way is up. A lack of clubs in the NWCL saw the bottom two divisions combined so that when the 1987/88 season kicked off the club was, at least, playing in the NWCL Second Division. It proved something of a false dawn. Of the 22 clubs, only Bacup Borough finished below the Dabbers. Nantwich had to go cap-in-hand to seek re-election to the league. Successfully gained, Peter Ward was appointed as joint-manager alongside Morris for the 1988/89 campaign.

THE LEAGUE MEN

Nantwich players who have gone on to feature in the Football League

Part 3: After the Second World War

Herbert Sandland (1953, Crewe 1 League appearance)
Alan Cooke (1955, Crewe 8)
Bobby Ryder (1965, Gillingham 8)
Stuart Sharratt (1966, Port Vale 143)
Bert Hulse (1967, Stoke 2)
Tony Cook (1981, Crewe 2 + 1 sub)
Jimmy Quinn (1981, Swindon 96+24,40 goals; Blackburn 58+13,17; Leicester 13+18,6, Bradford City 35,14; West Ham 34+13,18; Bournemouth 43,19; Reading 149+33,71; Peterborough 47+2,25; Northern Ireland)
Keith Thornhill (1983, Crewe 1)
Mark Came (1984, Bolton 188+7,7; Chester 47,1; Exeter 70,5)
Martyn Smith (1984, Port Vale 12+1,1)
Eddie Bishop (1988, Tranmere 46+30,19; Chester 97+18,28, Crewe 3)
Ronnie Jepson (1989, Port Vale 12+10; Peterborough 18,5; Preston 36+2,8; Exeter 51+3,21; Huddersfield 95+12,36; Bury 31+16,9; Oldham 9,4; Burnley 4+55,3)
Wes Wilkinson (2004, Oldham 2+4)
Matt Bailey (2004, Scunthorpe 2+2; Stockport 0+1, Crewe 0+2)
Simon Hackney (2005, Carlisle 78+37,17; Colchester 11+6*)

*Figure to end of 2008/09 season

CROWDED HOUSE ?

We've all heard the joke haven't we:
The phone rings at the old ground at Jackson Avenue.
"Hello, Nantwich Town Football Club."
"What time is kick off this afternoon?" asks the guy on the phone.
"What time can you get here, mate?" comes the reply.

Not true, of course – and neither is the quip that the crowd changes used to be announced to the teams over the PA (Come to think of it, the PA system at Jackson Avenue hardly ever worked properly anyhow!)

You get the gist, though. Attendances at the old ground weren't brilliant – yes, just 45 for that game against Bacup Borough in the North West Counties League in November 2003. Things are a bit different at the new Weaver Stadium and with the club's recent success, people in the town have really got behind the team – and given the club their full support. From being one of the worst supported clubs in the North West Counties League, the Dabbers are now one of the best supported in the UniBond Premier!

It's interesting to see how average home attendances have varied over the years (League matches only):

Season	Avg	Competition
1949/50	100	(Mid-Cheshire League – 5th)
1959/60	60	(Mid-Cheshire League – 15th)
1979/80	224	(Cheshire League – 14th)
1980/81	312	(Cheshire League – Champions)
1982/83	166	(North West Counties League Div.1 – Bottom)
1983/84	129	(North West Counties League Div.2 – Bottom)
2001/02	97	(North West Counties League Div.1 – 15th)
2002/03	99	(North West Counties League Div.1 – 6th)
2003/04	106	(North West Counties League Div.1 – 13th)
2004/05	85	(North West Counties League Div.1 – 16th)
2005/06	118	(North West Counties League Div.1 – 4th)
2006/07	285	(North West Counties League Div.1 – 3rd)
2007/08	502	(UniBond League Div.1 South – 3rd)
2008/09	664	(UniBond League Premier Div – 3rd)

TOP ATTENDANCES

For a Nantwich match:
14,647 1930 Cheshire Senior Cup Final v Macclesfield (at Crewe Alex), 12/4/30
Post-War:
4129 v Witton Albion, Cheshire Senior Cup 1st Rd 2nd replay (at Crewe Alex), 31/1/68

For a Home match:
Kingsley Fields (Temporary ground, 1919-1921)
5121 v Winsford United Cheshire Senior Cup 2nd Rd replay, 19/2/21

London Road/Jackson Avenue
4000 v Crewe Alexandra Reserves, Cheshire League, 21/4/24
Post-War:
League: 1536 v FC United of Manchester, NW Counties League Div 1, 24/2/2007
Cup: 2100 v Altrincham, Cheshire Senior Cup Quarter-Final, 18/2/67

Weaver Stadium
League: 1547 v FC United of Manchester, UniBond Premier League, 7/2/2009
Cup: 1783 v FC United of Manchester, FA Cup 1st Qual Rd, 13/9/2008

Jackson Avenue enjoyed its biggest post-war league crowd when FC United visited in February 2007

RISE AND FALL

At last, there was a more successful season. The Dabbers rose to fifth and, along the way, Ronnie Jepson notched 29 goals and clinched a transfer to Port Vale for a four-figure fee. Moreover, a number of NWCL clubs were promoted to the new First Division of the Northern Premier League. The club Committee had ensured that the old ground had been kept in pristine order despite the club's fall from grace. Their hard work now paid dividends as the excellent facilities at Jackson Avenue propelled the club to fill one of the vacancies in the NWCL First Division.

Restored to the NWCL top tier after an absence of six years, the Morris-Ward partnership steered the club to a creditable 7th place in 1989/90. Further proof of the club's renewal was acceptance back into the FA Vase in 1990/91 and the FA Cup the following season - competitions which Nantwich hadn't entered in the dark days of the late 80s.

The installation of floodlights had been anticipated for many years and they were now introduced at a cost of £20,000. A lot of hard work went into erecting those floodlights with the players, themselves, having to help carry the pylons into place. Such was their weight that it took 16 to 18 men to move them, one at a time!

For the 1991/92 campaign, Glyn Morris stepped aside, leaving Peter Ward in sole charge. Later to become Manager at Newcastle Town and Kidsgrove Athletic, Ward masterminded a run to the Third Qualifying Round of the FA Cup in the 1992/93 season. Maltby Miners Welfare, Congleton Town and Blakenhall were knocked out before

RONNIE JEPSON

As a teenager, Ronnie made a single Nantwich appearance in 1982/83 before joining Congleton Town. Re-joined Nantwich from Hanley Town at the age of 25 in the 1988 close season. Made a big impact, scoring 23 NWCFL goals and becoming club captain before signing for Port Vale in March 1989 for a £2000 fee. Had a loan spell at Peterborough United, before transferring to Preston North End for a £80,000 fee in February 1991. Moved on to Exeter City and then, in 1993, to Huddersfield Town for a £70,000 fee. Whilst with the Terriers, he formed a successful strike partnership with Andy Booth and earned the nickname Rocket Ronnie, firing his side to get promotion in 1995. He moved on to Bury, scoring a sensational goal against Millwall that set the Shakers on the way to the Second Division title in 1996/97, Oldham Athletic and Burnley where an achilles problem at the end of the 2000-2001 season ended his playing days. Appointed reserve coach at Turf Moor, he later became assistant and then Manager of Gillingham in November 2005 but parted company with the Kent outfit in September 2007.

INSTALLATION OF FLOODLIGHTS
April 1991
The first match under the new floodlights was a 2-0 win over Atherton LR on 30th April 1991 in the NWCL in front of a crowd of 84. Peter Hall scored the first goal under the lights. The floodlights were officially launched with a friendly match against Liverpool on 30th July 1991. A crowd of 1500 saw Liverpool win 1-0, courtesy of a Don Hutchison goal

OFFICIAL LAUNCHING OF FLOODLIGHTS AT JACKSON AVENUE
Nantwich Town F.C.
v
Liverpool F.C.
Tuesday, 30th July 1991 - Kick-off 7.30 p.m.
Admission by Ticket only   0050   Children & O.A.P.'s - £1

101

RISE AND FALL

Marine put the Dabbers out with an edgy 1-0 win at Jackson Avenue. Sadly, the Cup form hadn't been carried over into the league and with the Dabbers languishing in 20th spot, Ward resigned after a 3-0 defeat at Salford City in November.

Enter, stage left, Clive Jackson. A former British Rail train driver, Clive had been in charge of Nantwich's successful reserve team. Despite figuring for Crewe Alex's second string, Clive's own footballing career had been de-railed and, at 29, he became one of the league's youngest managers when appointed to take over the first team with Jon Brydon as his Assistant. He soon worked the oracle, picking up a Manager of the Month Award in February 1993 on the way to guiding the club to a respectable 13th position. For the first time, the club reached the Final of the North West Counties League Cup but, on the night, nerves got the better of some of the players on the big stage at Gigg Lane, home of Bury FC. 2-0 down at the break, a second half strike by Adrian Dunn proved nothing more than a consolation and the Dabbers went down 2-1 to Burscough.

Determined to wipe out that disappointment, 'Jacko' led the club to its highest North West Counties League placing, 4th, the following season. The campaign, though, was overshadowed by the tragic death of young centre forward Ryan Keen. Ryan had been a youth trainee with Crewe Alexandra before joining Nantwich in September 1993. He was a player with a bright future and had quickly become a Jackson Avenue favourite. He scored 11 goals in 25 appearances for Nantwich before his life was horrendously taken in February 1994 at the age of just 19. It was a terrible loss and not for the first time the club and supporters were left to mourn the loss of a promising young player. Memories were rekindled of April 1978 when outside left Keith Brookes had sadly lost his life in a car accident.

Perhaps it was a tribute to young Ryan that silverware was to follow when the Dabbers reached the League Cup Final in 1994/95. This time, Trafford were the opponents at Gigg Lane and the only goal of the game came from hitman John Scarlett. Captain Frankie Boon lifted aloft the cup and, for the first time in fourteen years, the door to the club's trophy cabinet creaked opened. Earlier in the season, Nantwich had been rocked by a couple of hefty cup defeats (10-0 at Northwich Victoria in the FA Cup and 7-1 at Hyde United in the Cheshire Senior Cup) but these were balanced

NORTH WEST COUNTIES LEAGUE CUP WINNERS 1994/95
The trophy that Nantwich captain Frankie Boon lifted in 1995 was originally used way back in 1893 as the Lancashire Combination League Cup, for which purpose it remained until 1982 when it was presented for use to the North West Counties League.

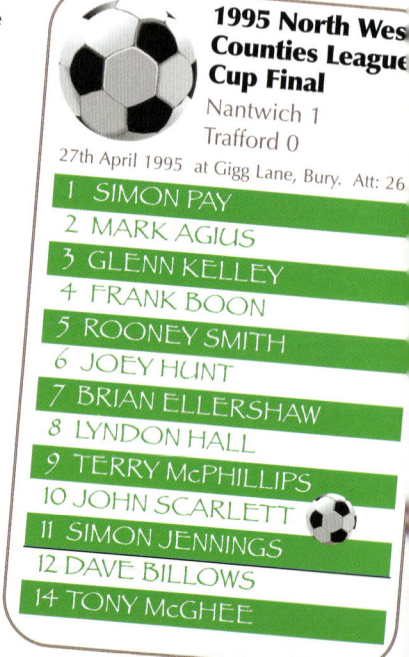

THE CARLING NORTH WEST COUNTIES FOOTBALL LEAGUE

CARLING LEAGUE CHALLENGE CUP FINAL 1994-95

NANTWICH TOWN
v
TRAFFORD

At Gigg Lane, BURY F.C.
Thursday 27th April 1995
Kick Off 7.30 p.m.

1995 North West Counties League Cup Final
Nantwich 1
Trafford 0
27th April 1995 at Gigg Lane, Bury. Att: 26_

1	SIMON PAY
2	MARK AGIUS
3	GLENN KELLEY
4	FRANK BOON
5	ROONEY SMITH
6	JOEY HUNT
7	BRIAN ELLERSHAW
8	LYNDON HALL
9	TERRY McPHILLIPS
10	JOHN SCARLETT
11	SIMON JENNINGS
12	DAVE BILLOWS
14	TONY McGHEE

MATCH OF THE DAY by Peter Hallett

Locke the key as Nantwich sail on

Peter had been asked by The Sentinel to report on what seemed to be a run of the mill FA Cup tie between Nantwich and Droylsden on 9th September 1995. Some years later, he put pen to paper to record his memories of that remarkable afternoon:

"I was hoping that the Dabbers would pull off a giant killing act against a team from a higher league. The game developed into a typical cup-tie with play end to end and both teams having chances - but it remained scoreless at half-time.

After the break, Droylsden stepped up a gear but they found the Nantwich defenders on top form and with The Dabbers forwards finding it hard to create a clear chance at the other end, the game appeared to be heading for a draw.

That is until the 82nd minute. Nantwich cleared the ball upfield. A quick passing move ended with Andy Locke cutting in and opening the scoring with a low left footed shot. I raced into the club's office and phoned through to The Sentinel, asking them to add to the bottom of my report that Locke had opened the scoring for Nantwich. I rushed outside to hear rapturous cheering from the Nantwich fans as the ball was being fished out of the net again. Locke had added a second goal by my watch on 83 minutes. I watched Droylsden kick off again but the Dabbers gained possession and raced upfield. The ball was played in to Locke and a teammate shouted for him to take it to the corner to run down the clock. Locke shaped to go that way but then cut inside in full flight and drove a great shot into the roof of the net. Unbelievable!! 3 goals in 2 minutes and 20 seconds.

I knew straight away that was a record for an FA Cup match and phoned the Sports Editor of The Sentinel. By 5.10pm, the headline in the Sentinel's old Saturday night football special, The Green 'Un, read "LOCKE THE KEY AS NANTWICH SAIL ON", with my opening paragraph, "Andrew Locke created FA Cup history when he netted the quickest ever hat-trick in the competition's history to sink Droylsden."

I had the scoop that many sports journalists dream about. The weekend was spent contacting FA statisticians to confirm the claim and also fielding phone calls from past players in various teams who had scored goals in FA Cup ties - but none had got a hat-trick in 2 minutes 20 seconds. I then contacted the Marketing Director of Littlewoods - the sponsors of the FA Cup at the time. Using their contacts, they got the BBC TV crews down to Jackson Avenue the following Wednesday evening for a midweek game. They interviewed myself and the Nantwich Secretary and broadcast it to some five million viewers. Then, the following day, they went to the school where Locke was a teacher and filmed him telling the pupils about how he had scored his hat-trick. So Nantwich Town became famous right across the nation.

For the record, the Nantwich team that day was Pay, Kelly, McGhee, Billows, Smith, Green, Ellershaw, Giblin, L.Hall, Murray, Locke. Subs: Brown, Heath, Glossop."

Peter Hallett was the Evening Sentinel's Non-League reporter for many years until his untimely death in September 2008. Peter was a familiar face around the local Non-League scene and a frequent visitor to Jackson Avenue. He had an insatiable appetite for football and an encyclopaedic knowledge of the beautiful game. He clocked up as many games in a season as most fans would in a decade but there is one that stood out in his memory above all others and which brought him - and Nantwich Town Football Club - into the national spotlight.

RISE AND FALL

**NANTWICH CHRONICLE
10 April 2001**
Manager Dave Cooke starts to make preparations for vacating the old ground at Jackson Avenue.

**NIGEL GLEGHORN
NWCL Manager of the Month
December 2003**
The Nantwich player-manager receives his award from NWCL Chairman Dave Tomlinson.

later in the season with two emphatic home wins in the league. Former Crewe Alexandra striker Terry McPhillips helped himself to a double hat-trick in the 10-0 trouncing of Skelmersdale United and by the end of the season had cracked home 40 goals. Not to be outdone, Scarlett also grabbed six goals a couple of months later in a 9-0 hammering of Bacup Borough.

The second half of the 1990s saw the Dabbers consistently finish in mid-table. Clive Jackson's increasing business commitments were making it impossible for him to continue as Manager. Moving 'upstairs' as club Chairman, he switched roles, retaining the Director of Football tag, whilst the managerial reins were passed to Paul Cuddy, Dave Cooke, Lester Norbury and Mark Gardiner (joint) and then former Stoke City and England midfielder Nigel Gleghorn. There was limited success on the field but a greater emphasis was placed on youth and nurturing the young footballing talent in the area.

It was off the field where momentum was now gathering. With the boom in house prices, the value of the Jackson Avenue site, relatively close to the town centre, had rocketed. The lack of car parking provision was becoming a major problem when big matches were on and the tight space around the ground prevented the development of further facilities needed by the club's burgeoning youth set-up. Gate receipts were not sufficient to cover the costs of running a team at North West Counties League level; a large function room was needed to bring in much needed revenue. With some reluctance, the decision was

RISE AND FALL

made to sell off the old ground and build a modern new stadium. A ground-share at Witton Albion's Wincham Park stadium for 1998/99 proved somewhat premature as legal and technical difficulties delayed the sale of the vacated Jackson Avenue and the club moved back 'home' for the 1999/2000 campaign.

By now Bernard Lycett had taken over as Secretary and a sub-group was formed of Chairman Clive Jackson, Vice-Chairman Jon Brydon and President Michael Chatwin, charged with moving forward the ground project. With the backing of the club Committee, the sub-group succeeded in securing a grant of £1million from the Football Foundation as well as pledges of £60,000 from Crewe & Nantwich Borough Council and £100,000 from Nantwich Town Council. As always with such matters there were further frustrating hitches, but finally the club's home of 123 years at Jackson Avenue was sold off to Barratts Homes and a new nine-acre site procured at Kingsley Fields.

The early years of the new millennium saw the club's youth set-up flourish. Bob Melling and Martin Stubbs were instrumental in the club becoming one of the first to secure the prestigious FA Community Club Charter Standard status.

Meanwhile, on the pitch, the players were responding to Gleghorn's astute coaching and, having struggled at the wrong end of the table for a number of seasons, the club sat comfortably in the North West Counties League. In November 2003, Gleghorn recruited former Crewe Alexandra and Burnley centre half Steve Davis to help shore up the defence. The veteran defender had had a short spell as Manager of Northwich Victoria but after that hadn't worked out, he was happy to resume his playing career at Jackson Avenue.

SIMON HACKNEY
The speedy winger was brought to Jackson Avenue by Nigel Gleghorn in November 2001. After terrorising NWCL defences, he stepped up to UniBond soccer with Woodley Sports. Transferred to Carlisle United for a £10,000 fee, he helped the Cumbrians gain promotion from the Conference in 2004/05 and then to League One. A six-figure fee took him to Colchester United in January 2009.

NANTWICH TOWN 1
TIPTON TOWN 0
18 October 2003
Jon Dawson shrugs off the challenge of Tipton's Melford Salmon in this FA Vase 1st Round tie as Mark Maguire looks on.

105

RISE AND FALL

The Dabbers finished the season in 13th place and when Gleghorn and the club parted company in the close season, Davis was appointed Head Coach under Director of Football, Clive Jackson. Not even the most ardent Nantwich fan could have predicted the success the club would enjoy over the next few years.

Former Nantwich striker Peter Hall, who had been helping to coach Port Vale's youngsters, returned to the club as Davis' assistant in January 2005. 'Hally', had been a prolific scorer in non-league football who started out with Parkway Clayton and originally joined the Dabbers from Macclesfield in 1988 becoming Nantwich's leading scorer in 1989/90 with 25 goals. After joining Newcastle Town in the 1991 close season he had returned to Jackson Avenue in October 1991 and topped the club scoring charts again that season and for the next two. He also turned out for Rists United, Eastwood Hanley, Burton Albion, Rocester, Shepshed and Kidsgrove Athletic. For that 2004/05 campaign, the Dabbers settled for a final placing of 16th in the North West Counties First Division but the foundations had been set for the club's rise.

**NANTWICH TOWN FC
2005/06**

National spotlight

*A*ll seemed quiet in sleepy South Cheshire as Steve Davis and Peter Hall readied their troops for the 2005/06 campaign. On 1st of October 2005, Nantwich visited West Midland League side Shifnal Town in the Second Qualifying Round of the FA Vase. Few in the crowd of 72 that afternoon could have anticipated where the Vase trail would lead for the club from the old market town.

The Dabbers had been exempt from the earlier qualifying rounds and a solitary strike from Mark Grice steered Nantwich into the next round. Young Rob Adlington secured a 1-0 win in a tempestuous game at home to Boldmere St Michaels in the First Round (Proper). Nantwich left back Danny Jarrett was dismissed for an off-the-ball incident in a match that saw three players sent off. Sometimes you feel the hand of fate on your shoulder and perhaps somehow it was destined to be the year for the Dabbers to get their hands on that prized trophy.

There was, of course, still a long way to go and the Second Round saw the Dabbers paired to visit Chasetown from the Midland Alliance. Charlie Blackmore's outfit were having a stomping season. Runaway leaders in the league, they had become the lowest ranked club to forge their way through to the First Round of the FA Cup that season. They had secured an impressive 0-0 draw away at Oldham Athletic and gave the Latics a scare in the replay before bowing out 2-1. Despite the recent exit from the Cup, the Staffordshire town was still buzzing from its club's Cup exploits when the Dabbers rolled in. Adverse weather had seen the tie postponed on the Saturday but on a cold Tuesday night, Nantwich turned the form book upside down and silenced the raucous locals with another hard earned single goal victory courtesy of former Crewe Alex youngster Matt Blake.

Stuart Scheuber secured a fourth consecutive 1-0 victory at Quorn and suddenly the Dabbers had equalled their previous best in the competition - a place in the fourth round.

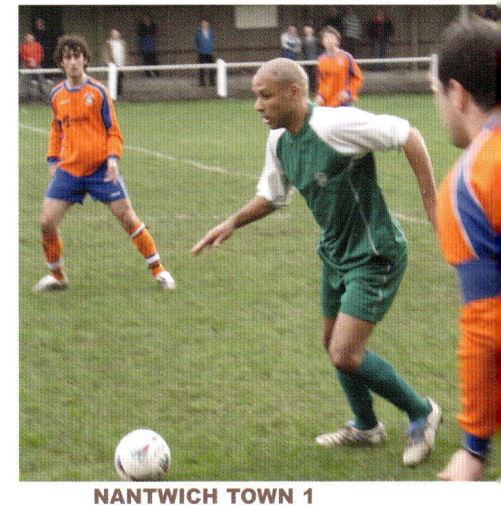

NANTWICH TOWN 1
BOLDMERE ST MICHAELS 0
FA Vase 1st Round
29 October 2005
John Scarlett takes on the Mikes' defence.

NATIONAL SPOTLIGHT

Again, Nantwich were required to travel - this time to deepest Suffolk to take on Needham Market of the Eastern Counties League. Leading 3-1 with ten minutes to go, it looked as though Steve Davis' men were through. But two dramatic late goals from the East Anglians took the tie to extra time. The Dabbers showed their determination and, against the odds, fought back to claim a 6-3 win.

There was a tough tie in store in the Fifth Round. Runaway Northern Counties East League leaders Buxton were drawn to visit Jackson Avenue. The Bucks brought with them a strong and loud following but another strike from Matt Blake gave the home side the lead against the run of play. Buxton threw everything at the Dabbers but the Nantwich defence held firm. Not even the award of a penalty could rescue Buxton as Rob Hackney got down to smoother David Reeves' spot kick and, after surviving another late barrage, there was huge relief at the final whistle. You didn't dare tempt fate and talk about it, but you just had that feeling it was going to be Nantwich's year.

NANTWICH TOWN 2
PICKERING TOWN 0
FA Vase 6th Round
12 March 2006
Danny Griggs is sent flying on the edge of the penalty area.

After the battle against Buxton, Pickering Town were less formidable opponents in the Sixth Round. Former Birmingham City midfielder and Cayman Islands international Martin O'Connor was drafted in to bolster the Nantwich line-up. His experience certainly paid dividends and a comfortable 2-0 home win saw the Dabbers through to the semi-finals.

Bookies favourites Cammell Laird were the team everyone wanted to avoid in the semis. But if Nantwich were to reach the Final it was going to have to be done the hard way as they were paired against the Wirral outfit. The first leg was scheduled for Rock Ferry and Steve Davis' tactics paid handsome dividends. The Nantwich midfield smothered the Lairds' engine room and when Matt Blake stole away to

CAMMELL LAIRD 0
NANTWICH TOWN 1
FA Vase Semi-Final 1st Leg
1 April 2006
Steve Davis sees off the challenge of Ian Cooke.

108

NATIONAL SPOTLIGHT

net a breakaway goal, the defence worked overtime to protect the lead. Even the most ardent Nantwich fan could hardly have dreamt of coming away from Kirklands with a first leg lead but the 1-0 victory meant the whole town eagerly anticipated the second leg eight days later.

The fellow North West Counties League side were running away with the league title and scoring goals for fun. Rumour has it that such was Laird's confidence of overturning the one goal deficit that champagne was placed on ice as the team coach rolled into South Cheshire. It was arguably the biggest match the old Jackson Avenue ground had staged and when the turnstiles clicked for the last time, there were 1320 packed into the ground.

Lairds made the early running and if a 10th minute strike by Lee Atherton had been inches lower, history could well have had a different tale to tell. As it was, the ball bounced off the crossbar and Nantwich gradually put the shackles on their maurauding visitors. When Andy Kinsey smashed the ball home in the 28th minute, such was the excitement that the pitchside barrier behind the goal buckled behind the weight of fans pushing forward to congratulate their hero. Adam Beasley's diving header just before the break made it 2-0 and when Kinsey added a third in the second half, Lairds knew their number was up. In the final few minutes, the sun shone through and it helped light up Nantwich fans as an exquisite lob from Stuart Scheuber nestled in the back of the net to record a famous 4-0 win. The pitch invasion that followed was reminiscent of that 25 years earlier when the Dabbers had clinched the Cheshire League title.

NANTWICH TOWN 4
CAMMELL LAIRD 0
FA Vase Semi-Final 2nd Leg
9 April 2006
Stuart Scheuber (arms raised) celebrates scoring Nantwich's fourth goal with Richard Smith and (no 3) Paul Taylor.

The one disappointment of the Vase campaign was that delays in the completion of the new Wembley meant that the 2006 Final would not, after all, be the first to grace the rebuilt national stadium. Instead, the FA had chosen Birmingham City's St Andrews ground to host the occasion. The opposition was to be Hillingdon Borough, of the Spartan South Midlands League, who had surprisingly overcome Bury Town in the Semi-Finals.

The old town buzzed with excitement as it anticipated the Final. Not since the club had first lifted the Cheshire Senior Cup over 70 years earlier was such a match so eagerly awaited. Tickets for the game were put on sale in the old canteen - they were snapped up like hot cakes. Hillingdon, on the other hand, were struggling to foster much interest in their exploits. By the time the Final came round, the opposition had sold only some 400 tickets. By contrast, almost 3000 Dabbers made the trip down the M6 and as the teams took to the field, a cacophony of cheers emanated from the sea of green and white. Former Leek Town striker Andy Kinsey led the team out in the absence of club captain Phil

NATIONAL SPOTLIGHT

NANTWICH TOWN

FA VASE WINNERS 2005/2006

FA VASE WINNERS 2005/06
Local photographer Tim Jervis brilliantly captured the magic of the FA Vase triumph. His stunning montage centres on club captain Phil Parkinson lifting the trophy and also features Steve Davis (top right), Danny Griggs (below right), Andy Kinsey (top left) and Adam Beasley (below left).

110

NATIONAL SPOTLIGHT

Parkinson. 'Parky' had cruelly turned over his ankle on an uneven pitch at Formby a week or so earlier. The ankle had ballooned up but, heavily strapped, he was not to be denied an appearance and entered the field of play as a second half substitute.

The spine of the team had moved en masse from Stone Dominoes in the summer of 2005 after the Staffordshire club's future had appeared to be in some doubt. Goalkeeper Rob Hackney, full backs Andy Taylor and Paul Donnelly, centre half Richard Smith and midfielder Stuart Scheuber were the former Doms' quintet. 39 year old Steve Davis partnered Smith at the heart of a defence that had kept a record breaking 8 clean sheets in the 9 games the Dabbers had played en route to St Andrews. Matt Blake, Phil Parkinson, James Marrow and Danny Griggs had all come through the youth ranks at Crewe Alexandra. Parkinson was in his second spell at Jackson Avenue after having also served Alsager Town and Newcastle Town whilst 'Griggsy' who had first appeared for Nantwich back in 1998 had tasted Conference football with Northwich Victoria. Hard working Adam Beasley was another former Newcastle Town man in the ranks.

The teams were presented to the FA's guest of honour Trevor Francis, the Birmingham City and England legend who had become Britain's first £1million footballer in February 1979. When the match got under way, the Dabbers quickly took a strangehold on the game and Hillingdon struggled to cope with the slick passing and off the ball movement. Stuart Scheuber cracked the post as early as the 4th minute and then, in the 13th minute, Blake turned the ball inside to Kinsey who wrong-footed his marker and fired from the edge of the penalty area to beat Ben Harris in the Borough goal.

Nantwich were now dominant and added a second on the half-hour when Griggs teed up Scheuber who slotted into the far corner of the net from just inside the box. Really, Nantwich's superiority should have given them more than a two goal cushion at half-time but, after the break, they extended their lead on 67 minutes. Hot shot Kinsey collected Blake's touch down and rifled home a 15 yarder which left Harris clutching at thin air. Racing over to the ecstatic Nantwich fans, Kinsey tugged off his green shirt but in throwing it into the crowd ended up dislocating his shoulder! He was unable to take any further part in the game. Veteran striker John Scarlett made a late substitute appearance for the Dabbers and, to their credit, Hillingdon didn't give up. They were rewarded with a late equaliser when substitute Leon Nelson bundled the ball over the line after Danny Tilbury's header bounced back off the upright.

There was no doubt who the winners were, though - Nantwich had proudly captured the FA Vase, the first side from Cheshire to do so. With captain for the day Andy Kinsey fetchingly draped in a pink blanket, Trevor Francis presented the trophy to club captain Phil Parkinson who lifted it aloft to cheers from the travelling green and white army.

THE FINAL COUNTDOWN
Head Coach Steve Davis (right) and Assistant Pete Hall (left) weigh up the Vase days before the Final. Chairman and Director of Football Clive Jackson didn't want to tempt fate by touching the trophy ahead of the match - but (below) was delighted to do so once it had been won!

2006 FA Vase Final

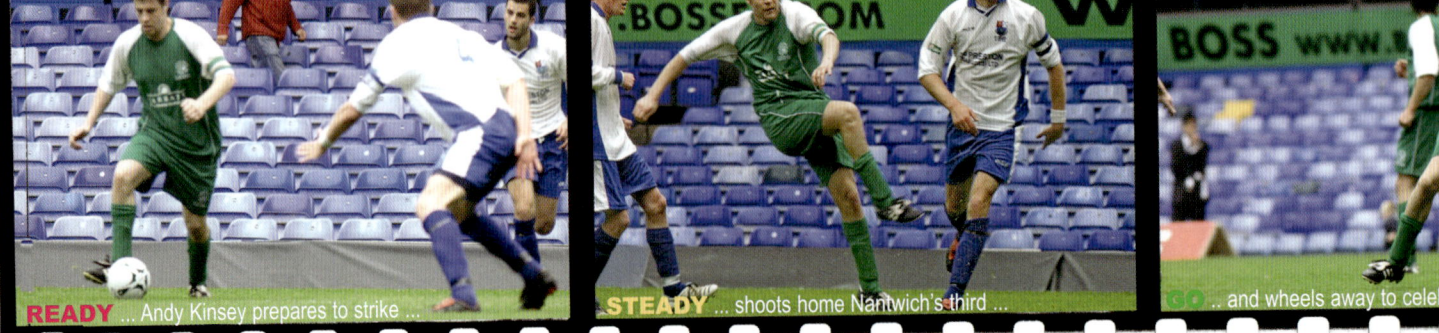

**Hillingdon Borough 1
Nantwich Town 3**

6th May 2006 at Birmingham City FC   Att: 3286

1 ROB HACKNEY
2 ANDY TAYLOR
3 PAUL TAYLOR
4 RICHARD SMITH
5 STEVE DAVIS
6 PAUL DONNELLY
7 ADAM BEASLEY
8 STUART SCHEUBER
9 ANDY KINSEY
10 MATT BLAKE
11 DANNY GRIGGS
12 PHIL PARKINSON — for 8, 70mins
14 JAMES MARROW — for 9, 70mins
15 JOHN SCARLETT — for 10, 87mins
16 MARTIN O'CONNOR
17 DANNY READE

The teams are led out and presented to guest of honour Trevor Francis.

Andy Kinsey fires Nantwich into an early lead.

READY ... Andy Kinsey prepares to strike ...
STEADY ... shoots home Nantwich's third ...
GO ... and wheels away to celebrate

The FA VASE FINAL 2006

Matt Blake takes on Hillingdon skipper Matt Kidson

...BUT dislocates his shoulder throwing his shirt into the crowd

Phil Parkinson holds aloft the Vase, flanked by Andy Taylor (left) and Danny Griggs

NATIONAL SPOTLIGHT

Arriving back in Nantwich, the players and supporters celebrated late into the night at The Leopard. The following days saw the club and players reflect on their achievement. There was unprecedented media attention and a Civic Reception in honour of the team was laid on by Nantwich Town Council. The players and officials paraded the Vase in an open top bus tour around the town - much to the delight of assembled fans and enthusiastic onlookers.

The achievement can certainly be put down as a defining moment in the club's long history but, by Monday evening, the Dabbers had to return to the bread and butter of the North West Counties League. There was still a fair chance of promotion but having to play three games in that final week of the season following the Vase Final proved too much. Steve Davis' side just missed out on promotion - having to content themselves with a 4th place that matched the club's best ever finish in the NWCL.

The euphoria of the Vase win was to prove the springboard for further success. The 2006/07 season was to be the emotional last campaign at Jackson Avenue and, having strengthened the team with the signing of Andy Bott, the former Newcastle Town and Stafford Rangers hotshot, a strong push for promotion was keenly anticipated. Sadly, there was an early exit from the Vase when visitors Shildon caught the holders on the hop in a thrilling Second Round tie, returning to the North East with a 4-3 extra time victory under their belts.

This time round, though, it was the league that was to be the focus of attention. The planned introduction of an extra regional division of the UniBond Northern Premier League meant that the top three sides of the NWCL would secure promotion. Rebel fans club FC United of Manchester and Curzon Ashton, themselves recently esconsed in their new Tameside Stadium, were going to be hard to catch but consistent performances saw the Dabbers maintain a top four position throughout the season. A record post-war league attendance of 1536 saw Andy Kinsey secure a vital point in a 1-1 home draw with FC United on 24th February but Nantwich were still running neck and neck with Salford City when Squires Gate visited for the last ever league game at Jackson

CELEBRATION 1
Players and officials celebrate winning the FA Vase aboard an open top bus parade around the town ahead of the Civic reception.

click4more

Watch a video clip of Andy Kinsey in the FA Vase Final.
Visit:
www.youtube.com/watch?v=Sb5wayPGKQ8&feature=related

CELEBRATION 2
28 April 2007
Promotion at last. Pictured after the final game of the 2006/07 season, a 2-1 win at Salford City, are:
Standing (left to right): Gyorgy Kiss, Steve Davis (Head Coach), Andy Kinsey, Danny Smith, Jake Bowyer, Adam Beasley, Mark Fitton, Richard Smith, Stuart Scheuber, Paul Donnelly, Bernard Lycett (Secretary), Paul Kelly (Physio), Clive Jackson (Chairman).
Crouching: Josh Hancock, Phil Parkinson, Paul Taylor, Andy Bott, Danny Griggs, Murray McCulloch, Peter Hall (Assistant Coach)

114

KING JOHN

When it comes to goals, there was nobody better than John Scarlett to find the back of the net for the Dabbers. 'Strap' is the Dabbers most prolific post-war marksman, netting over 160 goals for the Dabbers across 13 seasons (1993 to 2006).

It could have been even more but the 'Goal King' didn't join Nantwich until he was in his mid-20s. Having already served Middlewich Athletic and Haslington Villa, he progressed through the reserve ranks to make his Nantwich debut at Kidsgrove Athletic on 6th January 1993 in the Tennents Floodlit Trophy. It was a sign of things to come that he should score both goals in a 2-1 victory - and he scored in his next three games. Top scorer with 27 goals the following season, he tasted UniBond League football with Congleton Town in 1994/95, grabbing 8 goals in 16 league appearances. A fan of Liverpool (and Thai Boxing!), John was soon back bulging the net at Jackson Avenue. 38 strikes again made him the club's leading scorer in 1996/97 and a nominal fee took him to UniBond side Trafford in November 1997.

The lure of Jackson Avenue again proved too strong and, back on his happy hunting ground, John topped the scoring charts again in 1998/99 with 14 goals.

By the time he was in his mid-30s, John (who also notched 5 goals in a spell at Kidsgrove) was called upon less often.

However, the veteran striker, who served Mid-Cheshire League Crewe FC in the twilight of his career, could still be relied upon to find the back of the net - as he did in the FA Vase win at Needham Market en route to the Dabbers' 2006 FA Vase Final.

Fittingly, the veteran striker's farewell appearance in a green shirt was as a late substitute in the Vase Final at Birmingham City - and his FA Vase winners medal just reward for his fantastic service to the club.

john scarlett

Born Walsall, 5th August 1966
Height 6'0" **Weight** 11st 5lbs
Nantwich Career (Total: 161 goals)
1992/93 Goals 13 (7 Lge, 6 Cups)
1993/94 Goals 27 (15 Lge, 12 Cups)
1994/95 Goals 23 (20 Lge, 3 Cups)
1995/96 Goals 11 (9 Lge, 2 Cups)
1996/97 Goals 38 (29 Lge, 9 Cups)
1997/98 Goals 6 (5 Lge, 1 Cup)
1998/99 Goals 14 (8 Lge, 6 Cups)
1999/00 Goals 14 (11 Lge, 3 Cups)
2001/02 Goals 8 (6 Lge, 2 Cups)
2004/05 Goals 5 (5 Lge)
2005/06 Goals 2 (1 Lge, 1 Cups)

After service of almost a century and a quarter, the old Jackson Avenue ground off London Road staged its last Nantwich match for the visit of Squires Gate in the North West Counties League on 14 April 2007. A crowd of 1071 watched Nantwich win 5-2 thanks to goals from Andy Bott, Mark Fitton, Danny Griggs and Andy Kinsey (2). The club's special guest was Doris Hammersley - the daughter of William Chesworth who had been involved with the club since the 1880s and who commissioned the old grandstand back in the 1890s.

FAREWELL JACKSON AVENUE

Left: Artist Peter Greene's watercolour of the ground. **Right**: Andy Kinsey glides past the Squires Gate keeper in the final game whilst **(far right)** fans and players celebrate after the final whistle. **Above right**: The diggers move in as the stand and popular side are dismantled ready for the construction of the Keeper's Chase development.

Nick Brookes Demolition
JCB

Keepers Chase
A stunning development of 1, 2, 3 and 4 bedroom homes
BARRATT
www.barratthomes.co.uk
Call 01270 619343

NATIONAL SPOTLIGHT

Avenue. 1071 punters witnessed the occasion and the players responded to the carnival atmosphere with a 5-2 victory. An emphatic 4-1 midweek win at Bacup Borough gave the promotion drive further impetus and that all important third spot was secured on the Saturday in a tense 0-0 draw at Ramsbottom United. Salford's defeat to champions FC United of Manchester that afternoon gave the players and travelling fans cause to celebrate and the champagne fizzed open again as the club secured promotion to the UniBond League Division One South.

WEAVER STADIUM
July 2007
The new ground at Kingsley Fields was completed in time for the 2007/08 season - Nantwich's first season in the UniBond League.

With promotion coinciding with the much heralded move to the long awaited new £4m Weaver Stadium, the 2007/08 campaign would see support for the club mushroom. An inaugural friendly match against Port Vale at the new ground saw a 6-3 reverse in front of a crowd of 900. But the omens weren't looking too good when Quorn waltzed away with a 3-1 victory on the opening day of the season. However, attendances were proving far higher than at Jackson Avenue as the town and supporters wheeled behind the club, enjoying the plush new surroundings. In the space of a couple of seasons, Nantwich Town had gone from being one of the poorest supported clubs in the North West Counties League to one of the best supported in the UniBond League.

The faith of the new-found support was not misplaced and, having adjusted to the higher level of football and the splendour of their new stadium, the players found their feet. Impressive away wins at Hyde United and Northwich Victoria had set up an intriguing battle with rivals Cammell Laird in the semi-finals of the Cheshire Senior Cup. There were teething problems with drainage of the new pitch at the Weaver Stadium and after a couple of postponements, the Cheshire FA controversially switched the venue to Kirklands. Not to be outdone, the Dabbers put on a stirring display and second half goals from Ash Carter and Paul Taylor notched a workmanlike 2-1 victory and - with it - a place in the Final of the Cheshire Senior Cup for the first time in over 30 years.

The opponents were to be Altrincham, struggling near the base of the Conference; the venue, Witton Albion's Wincham Park; the date, April Fool's Day. Nantwich certainly weren't any fools on the night, though, and the nail biting Cup Final was as thrilling as the 5-4 victory over Runcorn back in 1976. On a heavily sanded pitch, Altrincham held a slender 1-0 lead at half-time, thanks to Chris Senior, but Nantwich were far from being outclassed by their more illustrious opponents - three rungs higher in the football pyramid. Shortly after the hour mark, former Crewe Alexandra striker Pavol Suhaj stepped off the bench. To say he made his mark on proceedings would be pure understatement. Within five minutes, he pounced on a loose

CHESHIRE SENIOR CUP WINNERS 2008
Supersub Pavol Suhaj celebrates the first of his amazing hat-trick.
Inset: Danny Griggs calmly seals victory in the penalty shoot-out.

2008 Cheshire Senior Cup Final
Altrincham 3
Nantwich Town 3 aet
Nantwich won 5-3 on penalties
1st April 2008 at Witton Albion. Att: 747

1	LEE JONES
2	PAUL DONNELLY
3	GYORGY KISS
4	RICHARD SMITH
5	PAUL TAYLOR
6	PHIL PARKINSON	108 mins
7	ASHLEY CARTER
8	GLYN BLACKHURST
9	ANDY KINSEY
10	ADAM BEASLEY	68 mins
11	DANNY GRIGGS
12	PAVOL SUHAJ	for 10
14	RYAN DICKER
15	NICK LINFORD	for 6
16	NATHAN SOUTHERN	for 12, 112 mins
17	MARK FITTON

Penalty scorers: Kinsey, Carter, Smith, Linford, Griggs.

PRIDE OF CHESHIRE
Standing (Left to right): Paul Kelly (Physio), Pavol Suhaj, Mark Fitton, Phil Parkinson (with trophy), Danny Griggs, Adam Beasley, Richard Smith, Lee Jones (at back), Ash Carter, Paul Donnelly, Andy Kinsey, Nathan Southern. Kneeling: Paul Taylor, Glyn Blackhurst, Gyorgy Kiss.

neville & albert

There have been few people over the years who have served Nantwich Town Football Club as faithfully as Neville Clarke and Albert Pye. Between them, the two close friends have filled virtually every role at the club, from Matchday Announcer and Gateman to Assistant Secretary and Chairman. Needless to say, both have been active Committee members and Trustees of the club.

Neville has supported the club since 1946 and, following in the footsteps of his father Harold, became a Committee man in October 1959 at the age of 25. In the 60s, Neville took charge of the youth team and guided them to considerable success. Like Albert, he has happy memories of the club winning the Cheshire Senior Cup in 1976 and being crowned Cheshire League champions in 1981.

"Above all else, winning the FA Vase in 2006 has got to be the greatest moment. It was fantastic," says Neville. And the worst? "It has to be the death of Ryan Keen not long after scoring the winning goal against Glossop in February 1994. Tragic, absolutely tragic."

neville's all-time nantwich XI

1 - Lee Jones
2 - Alan Bayley
3 - Bobby Ryder
4 - Paul Mayman
5 - Ron Siddall
6 - Alan Groves
7 - Micky Brookes
8 - Jimmy Fletcher
9 - Brian Griffin
10 - Johnny Walker
11 - Simon Hackney

Nantwich Town has been the love of Albert's life in more ways than one. As well as being dedicated to the football club, he met his wife-to-be, Olga at Jackson Avenue. Olga was, at the time, the manageress of the club canteen. Needless to say, their first date was a trip to Leek Town to watch Nantwich play!

Born in 1935, Albert became a Dabbers fan as a schoolkid and joined the Committee in 1966. Although he suffered a heart attack in 2001, a heart by-pass operation restored his health enabling him and Olga to continue their active involvement with the club.

Although neither Neville nor Albert has played for their beloved club, rumour has it that even now, in their 70s, their boots are ready and polished awaiting a call should they be needed to fill in for an absent player!

Here, Neville and Albert pick their all-time Nantwich side from all the players they have seen turn out for the club. "A very difficult task," says Albert. "Over the years there have been a heck of a lot of outstanding players in all positions."

1984 To mark the club's centenary, FA Secretary Ted Croker presents Albert Pye, Neville Clarke (centre) and Michael Chatwin with an illuminated address on the steps of the old FA headquarters at Lancaster Gate.

albert's all-time nantwich XI

1 - Lee Jones
2 - Frank Rhodes
3 - Kenny Cookson
4 - Kevin Roche
5 - Ted Neale
6 - Billy Hall
7 - Keith Mottershead
8 - Paul Mayman
9 - Brian Griffin
10 - Johnny Walker
11 - Simon Hackney

NATIONAL SPOTLIGHT

ball from Danny Griggs' corner to slam home an equaliser and then with just three minutes remaining he latched on to Kinsey's through ball to smack Nantwich into the lead. But, as was the case 30 years earlier, the travelling Nantwich hordes thought their moment of celebration had been denied when on-loan Stoke City defender Ryan Shotton pounced to net an injury time equaliser.

After the 90 minute whistle, Steve Davis and Peter Hall manfully rounded their troops and they were rewarded when the Slovakian majestically completed his hat-trick, a la Johnny Walker, feinting and turning past a bewildered Alty rearguard before driving past Stuart Coburn. 3-2 to the Dabbers but still Altrincham wouldn't lie down and a second goal from Shotton again levelled the scores on 107 minutes. Two minutes later, his work for the night done, a groin injury forced Suhaj himself to be substituted after the most impactive 44 minutes on the pitch you could imagine. Without 6'4" Pav's presence, Nantwich rarely threatened again and, when the final whistle blew, it meant a penalty shoot out would be required to decide who would lift the old silverware.

Where England have failed so miserably so often, Nantwich succeeded with aplomb. Nantwich's first four penalties all found Coburn's net and with Lee Jones having saved Alty's first spot kick by Jake Sedgemore, Danny Griggs stepped up to the mark and sent Coburn the wrong way to clinch a remarkable victory on another memorable night for the club.

"I'm very proud to have brought back the first piece of silverware to the Weaver Stadium," enthused Steve Davis. "Having been so close in normal time and then throwing it away, left me gutted. But, you only had to witness the body language of our players to see they weren't going to give up without a fight."

Having laid to rest the ghost of the Cheshire Senior Cup, the Dabbers were maintaining another promotion push in the league. It was all the more impressive given that this was the highest level of the national football

STEVE DAVIS
Head Coach
Born Birmingham, 26 July 1965, Steve is recognised as the most successful manager in the club's history, guiding the Dabbers to promotion from the North West Counties League and UniBond First Division South whilst capturing the FA Vase and the Cheshire Senior Cup. The former England Youth International originally joined Nantwich as a player in November 2003 stepping up to the role of Head Coach in the 2004 close season. The no-nonsense centre-half enjoyed a distinguished playing career which started as a trainee at Stoke City. He then served Crewe Alexandra, Burnley, Barnsley, York City (on loan), Oxford United and Northwich Victoria. Steve left the Weaver Stadium in June 2009 when he was appointed Assistant Manager at Crewe Alex.

pyramid at which Nantwich had played. A magnificent run in of 9 victories in the last 11 league games saw the Dabbers claim third place in the final reckonings. With champions Retford United out of the reckoning having failed ground grading requirements, runners-up Cammell Laird secured the automatic promotion slot. Nantwich were rewarded with home advantage in the play-off Semi-Final against Grantham and, after a lethargic opening, goals from Glyn Blackhurst and Andy Kinsey (who else?) saw a late turnaround and a play-off decider at home to Sheffield FC.

The world's oldest club wasn't going to give up the chance of promotion lightly - but then again neither were Nantwich. Twice Nantwich took the lead thanks to Glyn Blackhurst and Dave Walker but, in a near-repeat of the Senior Cup Final, they were again denied at the last when Robert Ward bundled a header past Lee Jones in the second minute of injury time. When a lacklustre extra time failed to provide any further goals, it was left to penalties to decide the final promotion place. Again, as in the Senior Cup Final, the Dabbers were faultless with their spot-kicks. Four out of four, so that when Sheffield's Mathew Lowton failed to beat Man of the Match Lee Jones, Nantwich secured their second promotion on the trot.

To have the outcome of a whole season of 40 or more matches decided by a handful of kicks from a penalty spot may seem cruel on Sheffield but the neutrals could not deny that, on the day, Nantwich deserved the victory - and, indeed, the visitors sportingly acknowledged that the Dabbers had earned their right to a place in the Premier Division of the UniBond League.

The 2008/09 season kicked off amidst much excitement. Steve Davis had again strengthened his squad, bringing in the prolific Michael Lennon from Kidsgrove Athletic to replace the departing Andy Kinsey and Pavol Suhaj. Former Macclesfield Town and Shrewsbury Town defender Darren Tinson joined from defeated Senior Cup finalists Altrincham and he would prove a rock in defence alongside former Port Vale youngster Charlie O'Loughlin. After defeat at Hednesford Town in their opening match, the new team blended well at the higher level and went the next eight league and cup matches undefeated. Amongst these was a thrilling 4-3 win at FC United of Manchester in a FA Cup replay, former Stafford Rangers front man Dave Walker helping himself to the match ball with a superb hat-trick. It followed a tense goalless draw which had set a record attendance of 1783 for the Weaver Stadium. Another new club, FC Halifax Town, were defeated in the Second Qualifying Round and after Lennon stole four goals in a 5-1 win at Whitley Bay, Nantwich found themselves in the Final Qualifying Round of the Cup for the first time since 1903. Unfortunately for the Dabbers, the Holy Grail of the First Round Proper of the FA Cup was again denied. A see-saw game in

NANTWICH TOWN 2
SHEFFIELD 2 (aet)
UniBond Division One South
Play-Off Final
3 May 2008
Adam Beasley rises above Sheffield's Jon Boulter. The Dabbers went on to win the penalty shoot-out 4-1.

Watch a video clip of the enthralling Cup tie at Fleetwood.
Visit:
www.youtube.com/watch?v=LjjfLhsttBw

TOP SCORERS

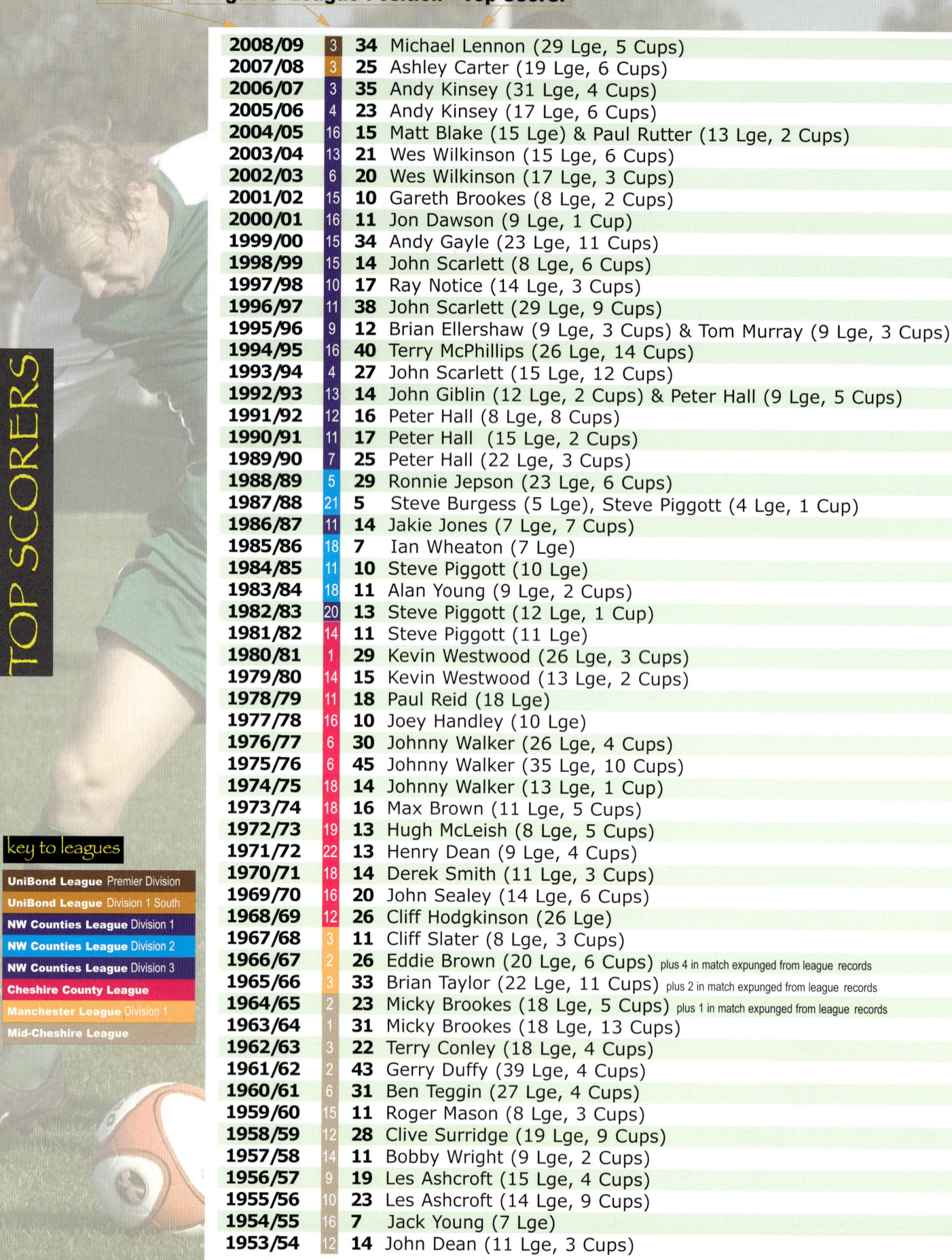

Season | **League & League Position** | **Top Scorer**

Season	Pos	Goals	Top Scorer
2008/09	3	34	Michael Lennon (29 Lge, 5 Cups)
2007/08	3	25	Ashley Carter (19 Lge, 6 Cups)
2006/07	3	35	Andy Kinsey (31 Lge, 4 Cups)
2005/06	4	23	Andy Kinsey (17 Lge, 6 Cups)
2004/05	16	15	Matt Blake (15 Lge) & Paul Rutter (13 Lge, 2 Cups)
2003/04	13	21	Wes Wilkinson (15 Lge, 6 Cups)
2002/03	6	20	Wes Wilkinson (17 Lge, 3 Cups)
2001/02	15	10	Gareth Brookes (8 Lge, 2 Cups)
2000/01	16	11	Jon Dawson (9 Lge, 1 Cup)
1999/00	15	34	Andy Gayle (23 Lge, 11 Cups)
1998/99	15	14	John Scarlett (8 Lge, 6 Cups)
1997/98	10	17	Ray Notice (14 Lge, 3 Cups)
1996/97	11	38	John Scarlett (29 Lge, 9 Cups)
1995/96	9	12	Brian Ellershaw (9 Lge, 3 Cups) & Tom Murray (9 Lge, 3 Cups)
1994/95	16	40	Terry McPhillips (26 Lge, 14 Cups)
1993/94	4	27	John Scarlett (15 Lge, 12 Cups)
1992/93	13	14	John Giblin (12 Lge, 2 Cups) & Peter Hall (9 Lge, 5 Cups)
1991/92	12	16	Peter Hall (8 Lge, 8 Cups)
1990/91	11	17	Peter Hall (15 Lge, 2 Cups)
1989/90	7	25	Peter Hall (22 Lge, 3 Cups)
1988/89	5	29	Ronnie Jepson (23 Lge, 6 Cups)
1987/88	21	5	Steve Burgess (5 Lge), Steve Piggott (4 Lge, 1 Cup)
1986/87	11	14	Jakie Jones (7 Lge, 7 Cups)
1985/86	18	7	Ian Wheaton (7 Lge)
1984/85	11	10	Steve Piggott (10 Lge)
1983/84	18	11	Alan Young (9 Lge, 2 Cups)
1982/83	20	13	Steve Piggott (12 Lge, 1 Cup)
1981/82	14	11	Steve Piggott (11 Lge)
1980/81	1	29	Kevin Westwood (26 Lge, 3 Cups)
1979/80	14	15	Kevin Westwood (13 Lge, 2 Cups)
1978/79	11	18	Paul Reid (18 Lge)
1977/78	16	10	Joey Handley (10 Lge)
1976/77	6	30	Johnny Walker (26 Lge, 4 Cups)
1975/76	6	45	Johnny Walker (35 Lge, 10 Cups)
1974/75	18	14	Johnny Walker (13 Lge, 1 Cup)
1973/74	18	16	Max Brown (11 Lge, 5 Cups)
1972/73	19	13	Hugh McLeish (8 Lge, 5 Cups)
1971/72	22	13	Henry Dean (9 Lge, 4 Cups)
1970/71	18	14	Derek Smith (11 Lge, 3 Cups)
1969/70	16	20	John Sealey (14 Lge, 6 Cups)
1968/69	12	26	Cliff Hodgkinson (26 Lge)
1967/68	3	11	Cliff Slater (8 Lge, 3 Cups)
1966/67	2	26	Eddie Brown (20 Lge, 6 Cups) plus 4 in match expunged from league records
1965/66	3	33	Brian Taylor (22 Lge, 11 Cups) plus 2 in match expunged from league records
1964/65	2	23	Micky Brookes (18 Lge, 5 Cups) plus 1 in match expunged from league records
1963/64	1	31	Micky Brookes (18 Lge, 13 Cups)
1962/63	3	22	Terry Conley (18 Lge, 4 Cups)
1961/62	2	43	Gerry Duffy (39 Lge, 4 Cups)
1960/61	6	31	Ben Teggin (27 Lge, 4 Cups)
1959/60	15	11	Roger Mason (8 Lge, 3 Cups)
1958/59	12	28	Clive Surridge (19 Lge, 9 Cups)
1957/58	14	11	Bobby Wright (9 Lge, 2 Cups)
1956/57	9	19	Les Ashcroft (15 Lge, 4 Cups)
1955/56	10	23	Les Ashcroft (14 Lge, 9 Cups)
1954/55	16	7	Jack Young (7 Lge)
1953/54	12	14	John Dean (11 Lge, 3 Cups)

key to leagues

- UniBond League Premier Division
- UniBond League Division 1 South
- NW Counties League Division 1
- NW Counties League Division 2
- NW Counties League Division 3
- Cheshire County League
- Manchester League Division 1
- Mid-Cheshire League

NATIONAL SPOTLIGHT

atrocious conditions at Fleetwood Town saw the Fisherman eek out a thrilling 4-3 victory. Nantwich had held the lead three times in the blood and thunder encounter but the hosts nicked victory courtesy of a goal two minutes from time. "I think we should at least have come out with a replay," said a dejected Steve Davis. It had been a wet and sorry sortie to the Fylde coast for the coachloads of Nantwich fans and it was a sad end to a brave Cup run for the Dabbers.

In a season of cup exploits, Nantwich also reached the First Round Proper of the FA Trophy for only the second time. It was 35 years since the Dabbers had last reached that stage of non-league's elite cup competition. Away wins at Frickley Athletic, Rugby Town and Warrington Town earned Nantwich yet another away trip in the First Round - a journey to Hednesford Town. As they did twice in the league campaign, the Pitmen came out on top, securing victory with a narrow 3-2 win.

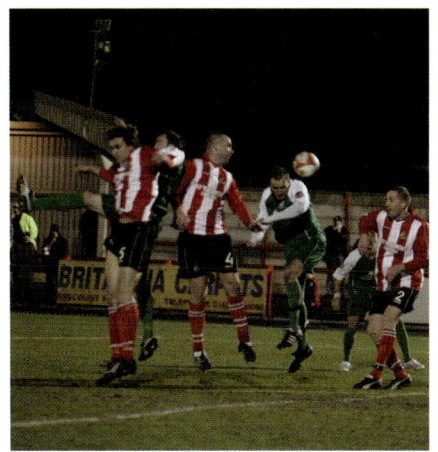

ALTRINCHAM 3
NANTWICH TOWN 0
Cheshire Senior Cup Final, 23 March 2009
Dave Whittaker gets amongst the Altrincham defence but the Blue Square Premier side proved too strong on the night in front of a crowd of 689.

Having waited 32 years to win the Cheshire Senior Cup, the Dabbers were not keen to let it from their grasp. Victories over Warrington Town and Woodley Sports saw Nantwich reach consecutive Senior Cup Finals for the first time in their history. And, would you believe it, the opponents and venue would be the same as last time round - against Altrincham at Witton Albion's Wincham Park. This time, the might of the Blue Square Premier side proved too strong and, on a blustery night, Alty gained revenge with a comfortable 3-0 victory.

Not to be outdone by the seniors' cup exploits, the Nantwich youth side went on a thrilling run in the FA Youth Cup. With Omar Mahmood and Nathan Southern firing goals for fun, Tony Ledwards' side brushed aside challenges from Salford City, Warrington Town, Wrexham and Curzon Ashton to set up a tie against League Two outfit Macclesfield Town at the Weaver Stadium. On the night, Nantwich were too strong for the young Silkmen and goals from Danny Edge and Nathan Southern secured a 2-1 win and the right to visit Goodison Park to take on the mighty Everton in the Third Round.

EVERTON 2
NANTWICH TOWN 0
FA Youth Cup 3rd Round
15 December 2008
The Goodison Park scoreboard shows Nantwich holding the Premiership youngsters but a 38th minute goal from Lewis Codling and an unfortunate own goal from captain Adam Dawson on 61 minutes, gave Everton victory.
Everton: Connor Roberts, Lee McArdle, Jake Bidwell, Moses Barnett, Shane Duffy, Hope Akpan, Thomas McCready, James Wallace, Lewis Codling, Conor McAleny, Nathan Craig. Subs: Aristote Nsiala, Gerard Kinsella, Karl Sheppard, Luke Powell, Georg Krenn.
Nantwich: Marcus Cooper, Jack MacKay, Elliot Ledwards, Josh Hancock, Adam Dawson, Danny Edge, Nathan Southern, Steve McNichol, Daniel Kirkham-Stubbs, Omar Mahmoud, Liam Prince. Subs: Shaun Turner, Ethan Tizard, Joshua Brehaut, Sam Proctor, Tom Parkes. Attendance: 797.

125

NATIONAL SPOTLIGHT

Memories were jogged of that disastrous night 56 years earlier when Nantwich's youngsters had been taught a footballing lesson by Manchester United's Busby Babes. But there was to be no repeat of that 23-0 thrashing. The young Dabbers performed admirably on the Premiership stage and, under the watchful eyes of first team boss David Moyes, the Toffees were made to work hard for their 2-0 win. The Nantwich youth players could be justly proud of their display against the Premier League stars of tomorrow and of the fact that they were the last non-league side to bow out of the competition.

EVERTON v NANTWICH TOWN
The splendid setting of Goodison Park

In the UniBond Premier, the Dabbers were playing at their highest ever level in the national pyramid set-up. To be around the play-off places for the bulk of the season was a massive achievement for the management duo and Director of Football Clive Jackson. As the season moved into the New Year, the team went on a run of 12 league games without defeat that even had people wondering if Nantwich could pip big-spending Eastwood Town to the title. It was not be to be, but a final league position of third secured home advantage in the play-off semi-final against Guiseley. A thrilling game on a late April evening went into extra-time and, eight minutes from time, Dave Walker slipped the ball past Piotr Skiba in the visitors' goal to clinch a berth in the Play-Off Final with a 2-1 win. It was Walker's 29th goal of the campaign and the man who had put Nantwich ahead was none other than Michael Lennon, whose tally of 34, made him the leading scorer in the UniBond Premier.

ILKESTON TOWN 2
NANTWICH TOWN 1
UniBond Premier Play-Off Final
2 May 2009
Michael Lennon strokes home Nantwich's first half equaliser.

Six coaches of Nantwich fans weaved their way towards Derbyshire as the Dabbers travelled to take on league runners-up Ilkeston Town in the Play-Off Final. Ilkeston themselves had needed extra-time to dispose of Kendal Town in their semi but on a bright afternoon, both sides looked nervous with a place in the Blue Square North awaiting the winners.

The home side struck first when Ben Pringle stabbed home from close range on 10 minutes but the prolific Lennon levelled matters on the half-hour when he seized on a backpass and nutmegged keeper Chris Adamson to roll the ball into an empty net. With both sides struggling to find top gear, Ilkeston had Anthony Church sent off for throwing a punch at centre-half Charlie O'Loughlin. It later emerged that the former Port

126

NATIONAL SPOTLIGHT

Vale youngster had played the match despite being unwell and, the following day, was admitted to hospital to have his appendix removed. The Dabbers, though, struggled to make the extra man count and early in extra-time, Ilkeston captain Simon Weaver headed past Lee Jones to make it 2-1. Jones was also playing through the pain barrier enduring severe back spasms but he heroically threw himself at substitute Amari Morgan-Smith's late penalty to keep Nantwich hopes alive. Sadly, there was to be no happy ending this time with the Dabbers being denied a third promotion on the trot. Nevertheless, the 500 travelling Nantwich fans applauded their side off their field in appreciation of their hard-working efforts over a long season.

Ironically, Ilkeston's goalscoring heroes both left the club shortly afterwards. Man of the Match Pringle was snapped up by Derby County whilst the experienced Weaver was appointed Manager of Harrogate Town. Both clubs were also to lose their managers. Ilkeston's Rob Scott and Paul Hurst became joint-managers at Boston United whilst Steve Davis took up the post of Assistant Manager at Crewe Alexandra. There was further irony when Nantwich's Charlie O'Loughlin switched to Ilkeston during the close season.

After decades in the doldrums, the fans knew that the Dabbers were approaching their 125th anniversary celebrations on the crest of a wave. All those who have put time and effort into the club since 1884 would be proud of what has been achieved in recent seasons. But in celebrating this success, we should pay testimony to those whose sweat and toil over the course of the club's long history has kept Nantwich Town FC afloat, often in difficult times. Fans of today can now enjoy the rewards. In the words of the matchday chant which echoes around the Weaver Stadium, we remember all those stalwarts from yesteryear who were also "Proud To Be A Dabber".

CHARLIE O'LOUGHLIN
The Nantwich centre-half is crowded out in the Play-Off Final at Ilkeston.

DANNY GRIGGS
Nantwich's second highest post-war goalscorer, 'Griggsy' netted 114 goals after making his debut at Workington on 12th November 1998. The former Crewe Alex youngster interspersed his time at Nantwich with spells at Mossley, Middlewich Athletic, Newcastle Town and Northwich Victoria. He left the Weaver Stadium for Congleton Town in July 2009.

GREEN & WHITE ARMY
Nantwich's travelling supporters salute their side at Ilkeston ... "If you're proud to be a Dabber, clap your hands" ...

acknowledgements

I am grateful for the help given by many people in the compilation of this book. Without their assistance, it would not have seen light of day. There are many individuals who have been supportive and, in particular, I would like to thank the following:

Associated Sports Photography, Peter Barnes, Peter Bebbington, Bob Bickerton, John Brough (www.dabbersnantwich.me.uk), Neville Clarke, Keith Clayton, Gary Cliffe, Ronnie Cope, Paul Cowburn, Gordon Davies, Pat Elliott, English Heritage (NMR Aerofilms Collection), Harold Finch, Geoff Findlow, John Fitzhugh, Kevin Hammersley, Chris Harper (The Sentinel), Bert Hulse, Alan Jervis, Tim Jervis (timjervisphoto.co.uk), Phil Johnson, Bryn Jones, Tim Lees, Brian Lindop, Michael Joyce (www.since1888.com), Ian McDonald, Peter Morse (Nantwich Chronicle), John Nicholls, Judith Parkes, Albert Pye, Harry Simpson, Neil Southern, Paul Springthorpe & Rob Tilley (The Printing House, www.theprintinghouseltd.co.uk), Chas Sumner, Mike Talbot, Chris Williams as well as the staff of Crewe Library and Nantwich Library.

I must also thank my partner, Nichola, and our young daughter Ruby Angel who have shown great patience in allowing me to endlessly spend hour after hour researching and typing away on my computer.